Praise for
Because I Knew You Were Mine

"This is an incredible story about personal resilience, an indomitable spirit, and finding great purpose. Through God's grace, Patricia has overcome devastating childhood trauma and overwhelming adult hardships to find a life full of purpose, joy, and generosity."

—William "Bill" Bedrossian, MSW
President & Chief Executive Officer
Covenant House International

"We all live with our memories. Some are soft and sweet; some are painful and hard. Our lives are shaped by these memories. Pat Stroberg grew up with deep, hurtful memories which could have kept her stuck in pain for the rest of her life. She chose, however, to focus on what she could do to move out of the darkness into the light. In this book, she shares with us how we can move into a full and joyous life no matter how painful our past has been. We have the ability to choose how our memories control how we live our lives. If the time comes when we get stuck by our past memories, this book can help us move through the darkness into the light. I hope others find this book as helpful as I have."

—Gladys T. McGarey M.D., M.D.(H)
Author of *The Well-Lived Life*

because i knew you were mine

mine

a memoir of forgiveness

PATRICIA STROBERG

BERRY POWELL PRESS

Because I Knew You Were Mine: A Memoir of Forgiveness

Copyright © 2024 by Patricia Stroberg
All rights reserved. No part of this publication in print or electronic format may be reproduced, stored in a retrieval system, or transmitted in any form or by any means, electronic, mechanical, photocopying, recording, or otherwise without the prior written permission of the publisher except for use of quotations in a book review.

First paperback edition March 2024
Cover Design by Kay McConnaughey
Interior Design by Formatted Books
Published by Berry Powell Press
Glendora, California
www.berrypowellpress.com

ISBN: 978-1-957321-14-1 (paperback)
ISBN: 978-1-957321-15-8 (ebook)
Library of Congress Control Number: 2023924380

The people and events in this book are real and are recounted from the author's memory. Some names have been changed to protect individual privacy. The author of this book does not dispense medical advice or prescribe the use of any technique as a form of treatment for physical, emotional, or medical problems without the advice of a physician, either directly or indirectly. The intent of the author is only to offer information of a general nature to help you in your quest for emotional, physical, and spiritual well-being. In the event you use any of the information in this book for yourself, the author and the publisher assume no responsibility for your actions.

Dedication

This book is dedicated to Covenant House.
There, but for the grace of God, go I.
Fifty percent of my profits from my book sales will go to Covenant House.

Acknowledgments

Capturing memories and committing them to my journal has been a routine task since I was a young girl. Over the years, I have written thousands of pages filled with decades of memories that include the severe neglect and trauma I suffered as a child.

When I reflected back on my journals in my late seventies, I became deeply aware that my life had been saved by grace. Time and again, I've sensed an angel on my shoulder guiding me toward people capable of loving me in powerfully healing ways. I believe my purpose now is to share how God has helped me overcome my circumstances rather than remain trapped in a sense of victimization. It wasn't until I entered my eighties that I decided to write my memoirs.

But writing in a journal and becoming a published author are very different journeys. I needed guidance and assistance, which was provided by the talented team at Berry Powell Press. I am grateful to Carmen Berry, co-founder of Berry Powell Press, who helped me link stories and articulate meaning to my recollections. In addition, my book coach, Marianne Croonquist, transcribed my handwritten journal entries into the computer, and together, we sifted through memories, storylines, and insights. The three of us shared many rounds of laughter, cups of hot tea, and hard conversations to pull together the stories that best expressed my journey.

I want to give a special shout-out to the editing talents of Valeri Mills Barnes, Abigail Dengler, and Kathleen Turner. Kay

McConnaughey worked magic, creating a phenomenal cover from an old, faded, creased, and damaged photograph. Carolyn Rafferty made a way to enhance additional photos of my past so that they could be included in this book. Our creative partnership made it possible for me to write my two memoirs.

Lady, You Got Balls: The Gift of Being Underestimated, published in 2020, was written to encourage and empower women entrepreneurs who dream of successful business careers yet face discrimination due to their gender. I co-founded a manufacturing company in the late 1970s when the industry was dominated exclusively by male executives. My first book unveils my progression through a troubled childhood, naïve young love, and a troubled marriage that blessed me with a wonderful son yet ended in divorce. With the help of mentors and a sustaining faith, I overcame the obstacles to own and lead a highly competitive company.

Because I Knew You Were Mine, my second memoir is written for those who have known the overwhelming pain of childhood neglect or trauma. This story delves into the secrets I uncovered about my extended family—most significantly involving my mother's mental health challenges. My father, reliable yet emotionally stoic, was unable to shield me from the realities of their turbulent relationship. My book shows that it's possible to overcome dire circumstances of deprivation and abuse and how to break free from toxic relationships.

When I was thirty-two, I discovered Covenant House. I was moved by their recognition of young people who need help, resourcing, and a place to belong. Realizing that I shared many of the wounds of those they served motivated me to start donating regularly to their work—just two dollars a month. As my company grew and my personal resources expanded, I was able to contribute more and become part of their community.

In particular, I want to acknowledge Bill Bedrossian, Amanda Sattler, and Tom Bagwell, who have been great friends through the years. May Covenant House, their staff, and those served by them know they have influenced the message in this book and provided purpose to my story. I applaud Covenant House and thank them for their inspiration and for giving purpose to my words. I am grateful if any part of my sharing can provide validation, hope, or purpose to the pain others know. To honor their work, I am sharing half of the royalties from the sales of this book with Covenant House.

I also want to acknowledge Dr. Gladys McGarey who has been my doctor, mentor, and friend since 1991. Her influence has forever changed my life and spirit.

I am grateful to my therapist, Vanessa, whose brilliant insight and unfailing confidence in my healing ability gave me the guidance and support required for transformation. My former neighbor, Dorothy, was one of my dear friends who emboldened me to stick up for myself when I felt beaten down.

I am thankful for the friends at Bridge, my church choir, and travel companions who have joined me on numerous international adventures. I am also grateful for my long-time friend and neighbor, Sophie.

Lastly, I want to honor my dear dogs, Conrad and Osso, who both passed away while I was writing this memoir. Their companionship and love goes beyond words. I am grateful for Kandy, my new dog, who joins me at the table each morning while I read the paper.

Contents

Chapter 1	Who Is My Mother?	1
Chapter 2	I'm a Big Girl Now	7
Chapter 3	Blackouts in Ohio	13
Chapter 4	I Have a Father?	17
Chapter 5	We're Going to Be a Family	23
Chapter 6	You're Not the Mommy I Want	31
Chapter 7	Sunday, the One Day of Joy	37
Chapter 8	Cocoa and Toast	41
Chapter 9	Why Don't You Believe Me?	45
Chapter 10	Is My Mother Dying?	51
Chapter 11	I Don't Want a Little Brother	55
Chapter 12	I Wish I Could Fly Away	59
Chapter 13	The Fur and the Fire	63
Chapter 14	Why Are We Living in a Hospital?	69
Chapter 15	Pork Chops on the Stove	73
Chapter 16	I Don't Want You Either	79
Chapter 17	Moms for Hire	87
Chapter 18	You Missed Your Chance	95
Chapter 19	Starting New in California	99
Chapter 20	Is There Hope?	105
Chapter 21	When I Marry, My Life Will Be Perfect	109
Chapter 22	Who Will Walk Me Down the Aisle?	131
Chapter 23	And Baby Makes Three	135
Chapter 24	Broken Hearts Club	141

Chapter 25	You Will Do the Right Thing	145
Chapter 26	Amazing Grace	151
Chapter 27	Pork Chops on the Stove Again	157
Chapter 28	I Married My Mother	163
Chapter 29	Mom, I See What They Do to You	169
Chapter 30	Missing Puzzle Piece	175
Chapter 31	Because I Knew You Were Mine	179
Chapter 32	A Choice, a Response	187
Chapter 33	She Should Have Been Locked Up	193
Chapter 34	Mother-Daughter Bond?	201
Chapter 35	We Were Alike	207
Chapter 36	Disappointment and Loss at Forty-Three	213
Chapter 37	This Woman Is in Charge	219
Chapter 38	Things Turn Around	227
Chapter 39	Enough Isn't Enough for Everyone	233
Chapter 40	I Forgive You	241
Chapter 41	Peace, Finally	245
Chapter 42	To You, My Reader	255

Epilogue 263
About the Author 267
Note from the Publisher 269

Who Is My Mother?

The year was 1943. I was three years old, standing on my tiptoes and clutching the arm of a wooden rocker so I could get a look at the face of a new baby girl held lovingly in Aunt Gertrude's arms. The baby had a delicate blonde fringe that framed her small, pudgy face and smelled like soap and powder. Uncle Alvar stood behind me, with his chest puffed out the way fathers do at the sight of their progeny. Filling the air with smoke, he puffed on a cigar, one of the few remaining after he'd passed them out to anyone who was willing to take one. On the other side of the rocker was Gramma Stroberg, the family matriarch, sitting in her armchair, cooing and grinning.

Our baby is here!

Wiping her hands on her apron, Gramma gently touched Marilyn's newborn face. "Isn't it wonderful, Gertrude? You have a daughter. You are officially a mother."

Aunt Gertrude, perched in the rocking chair in the clean and tidy room, beamed down at the angelic little face. "Make sure your first word is Mama." She looked up at her husband and winked. "Although Dada is okay too."

He chuckled.

Those were the days of "children should be seen and not heard," and adults talked over me—literally.

Somehow, my young brain realized that if Marilyn's arrival made Aunt Gertrude a new mother, then Aunt Gertrude wasn't *my* mother, even though she was the only mother I'd ever known.

No one had ever told me Aunt Gertrude was my mother, but who else could she be? She raised me as her own. And I looked just like her. We both had blue eyes and strawberry-blonde hair. So, in my heart, Aunt Gertrude was my mommy. The fact that I called her Aunt Gertrude, not Mommy, was a distinction that hadn't been clear to me up to this point.

I crawled into Gramma Stroberg's lap for comfort. I loved to sit on Gramma's lap. She smelled like Pond's cold cream and would wrap her thin arms tightly around me so I could cuddle. I studied her face and hair—the same blue eyes, and even though she had gray streaks through her hair, it was strawberry-blonde like mine and Aunt Gertrude's. I looked up at her face and whispered, "Are you still my grandmother, Gramma?"

"Of course, Patsy!" she said with surprise in her eyes. She looked over at Aunt Gertrude. "Why on earth would she ask something like that?"

Aunt Gertrude shrugged and went back to adoring baby Marilyn. I buried my face in Gramma Stroberg's arm and felt ashamed for asking. My little brain reviewed the information I had. Aunt Gertrude wasn't my mother, but Gramma Stroberg was still my grandmother. *Somehow, I belong here, but not quite.*

Somehow, I belong here, but not quite.

Uncle Alvar put his hand lovingly on Marilyn's head and smiled. He had never smiled at me like that, nor had I wanted him to. He was stiff with a gruff manner and distant in his ways. In fact, I could tell he didn't much like having me around. Looking back, I see that even though

I had mistaken Aunt Gertrude for my mother, it never crossed my mind that Uncle Alvar could have been my father.

I was pulled out of my confusion when a knock sounded at the front door. Gramma gave Aunt Gertrude a disapproving glance. "That's probably the Davis family."

"Why would they come over now?" Aunt Gertrude sighed.

Gramma shrugged while Uncle Alvar opened the door to the familiar and distinct chatter of Grandma Davis and the heavy footsteps of Grandpa Roy. I was delighted to see Grandma Davis. Grandpa Roy was a different matter. Uncle Alvar gestured toward baby Marilyn, then stuck his head out the door to search the porch. "Did Betty come with you?"

Grandma Davis ignored his question. Her brown hair, cut short and curled, floated across the room, arms stretched to show off her rabbit fur coat at its best advantage. Her face, round and red from the cold, pulled into a wide, cheerful grin. "Oh, Gertrude, let me see your new baby!"

Aunt Gertrude didn't look pleased as Grandma Davis swooped in and scooped Marilyn into her arms. Grandpa Roy stayed close to the front door as if being kept against his will, anxious to escape at the first opportunity. He wore his usual wrinkled shirt and work pants, was unshaven, and cast an unsavory smell of cigarettes and cheap alcohol. No one invited him in further, perhaps relieved by his distance. A poorly wrapped present was in one hand and a smoldering cigarette in the other.

"She is beautiful!" Grandma Davis cooed, kissing the baby on the cheek. She looked at Aunt Gertrude, smiling. "I'm so happy for you!"

Aunt Gertrude stood up, taking Marilyn back as politely as possible. "Thank you, Jeanette."

Grandma Davis turned to her husband. "Hand me the present, Roy! Where're your manners?" He obeyed, leaning toward her rather than walking further into the room. Taking a final drag, he opened the front door and tossed the butt outside, letting in a blast of freezing air.

Grandma Davis smiled again as she put the present on the coffee table. "It's not much. You know, with the war and all. But we saved up some of our ration coupons and got the baby a little something."

Gramma Stroberg set me down as she got up to retrieve the present. "That's so kind of you. There was no need for you to go out of your way."

"Well…" Grandma Davis's voice trailed off as if that was not a sufficient reason for her generosity. I sensed a tension in the room. I had no way of knowing that I, as the connecting factor between the two families, was the source of it.

As if to change the topic, Grandma finally looked down at me. "Patsy! Isn't this exciting? You'll have someone to play with now!" I held out my hands to Grandma Davis, whose tiny frame picked me up. "Oh, you're getting so big, Patsy!"

Uncle Alvar pulled a chair up behind her. "Here you go, Mrs. Davis. Would you like me to take your coat?"

Pulling it tighter, she said, "Oh, no!" She plopped down into the chair with me in her arms, and I laid my head on her coat, feeling the soft fur and resting in her comfortable embrace as the two families struggled to make small talk.

The Strobergs and Davises were as different as two families could be. My father's side of the family was Swedish, stoic, financially stable, and rigidly bound by duty. My mother's family had suffered severely during the Depression, losing their home and belongings, and they might have starved had it not been for the bread lines. Yet through it all, my Irish Grandma Davis had refused to sell her rabbit coat. It was her most prized possession, and she proudly wore it all winter long.

Uncle Alvar continued his role as host, pointing to a chair near Grandpa Roy. "Would you like to sit over there?"

Roy stayed by the door. "I'm fine here."

Uncle Alvar stood awkwardly, not knowing if he should stand in solidarity with Grandpa Roy or sit. In frustration, he blurted out, "Well, we've not seen Betty for some time."

"Alvar!" Aunt Gertrude scolded him. Baby Marilyn was startled in her arms.

"It's okay, Gertrude," Grandma Davis said sadly. "We haven't seen her either."

Gramma Stroberg intervened. "Gertrude, let me hold the baby. Why don't you open their present!"

The conversation continued overhead as I snuggled further into the comfort of the fur coat. This Betty they talked about was of no interest to me. I'd only seen her a few times—a dreary, sad woman with bright lipstick who never spoke to me. My connection was only with my Grandma Davis, who had forged an unsteady peace with the Strobergs so she could visit me, her only grandchild.

A wave of concern swept through my heart. I whispered the same question to Grandma Davis. "Are you still my grandma?"

She laughed and looked down at me with a similar confusion I'd seen on Gramma Stroberg's face. "Oh, yes, dear Patsy. I will always be your grandma. No matter what."

I relaxed in her lap, feeling safer and relishing her warmth. Two grandmothers, one in her functional apron and one in her beloved fur, belonged to me, and I belonged to them. That was something to hold on to.

I was nervous the first few days after Marilyn came to live with us, but before long, I calmed down since everything stayed the same. We continued living on one side of a set of two-bedroom duplexes. Marilyn's crib was put into Aunt Gertrude's and Uncle Alvar's room, and Gramma Stroberg and I still shared the second room. On the other side of the duplex lived a friendly family with a girl close to my age that I played with sometimes. Apparently, they weren't related to us at all. Yet, there was still a bit of confusion and fear in the pit of my stomach. *If Aunt Gertrude isn't my mother, who is, and where is she?*

I'm a Big Girl Now

The war in Europe was in a desperate state, and in 1944, Uncle Alvar joined the Army. After that, Aunt Gertrude cried a lot, and the grandmothers were on hand to comfort her.

I remember afternoons when we were all gathered around the kitchen table—a family of five females if you count me on Grandma Davis's lap and Marilyn in Aunt Gertrude's arms. The grown-up ladies had a somber discussion about the general state of the world and theirs in particular.

Gramma Stroberg was clearly the matriarch of the group. She would have been even if she hadn't been a bit older than Grandma Davis, probably due to the sheer power of her character and the strength of her Lutheran faith. A stoic Swede with her back straight and chin held high, Gramma Stroberg wore her graying blonde hair carefully cut and coiffed. She held her emotions as tightly as her posture. She was rarely prone to emotional displays.

But Gramma Stroberg had to be a strong woman. Widowed when her third child, Al, was only six weeks old, she sought financial help from the Ohio government. They offered her a stipend only if she agreed to place the infant in an orphanage. Determined to keep all her children with her, she refused. She had just lost her husband; she was not going to lose her newborn son too. She made a sparse living, cleaning, washing, sewing, and cooking for families. Little Al came with her and was placed in a laundry basket while she worked.

Aunt Gertrude was also keenly aware of her responsibilities and duty. She did her best to keep her feelings in check as she unpredictably remembered that she was a new mother with a husband in the battle against the Nazis. She dabbed her eyes with a pink cotton handkerchief as she spoke. "I worry so much about him." She paused to gather herself. "And Al, too, of course."

"Of course you do. You've got your husband and your brother both in the war. It is a lot for us all to withstand. But the good Lord is watching out for all of us. Let's remember that." Gramma Stroberg's validation and faith temporarily soothed the collective nerves. She spoke of Al on the ship fighting in the Pacific. "You know, I haven't gotten a letter from him in a couple of weeks," she said softly. She turned to Grandma Davis. "Has Betty gotten word from Al?"

Grandma Davis, the third part of this female trinity, was also a force to be reckoned with. She had the courage to insist on taking her rightful place as my grandmother, although at the time, I had no clue as to how she was related to me. She shrugged sadly. "Betty never tells me anything. Most of the time, I don't know where she is." Everyone looked down at that point as if making eye contact was too revealing. No one noticed that I was all ears.

One cold morning, Aunt Gertrude pushed the stroller with one hand, Marilyn tucked snuggly inside, and her other hand held tightly to mine. We walked from the biting winter air into the warm cocoon of the nursery school. Taking off our coats and hats, I sensed that I'd been there before, but the memories were hazy.

The big room was clean and colorful; all the children sat quietly in a circle, their hands in their laps, listening to a story. The teacher, smiling and welcoming, saw us and pointed us toward a side office. Before we could make it all the way across the room, a thin woman with a tight bun in a navy blue suit came out of the office and met us halfway.

She looked down at me and smiled. "Hello, Patsy." I smiled back. *How does she know my name?*

By the time she made eye contact with my aunt, her face was stern. "I'm Mrs. Peterson, the preschool director."

My Aunt introduced herself. "I'm Mrs. Johnson, Patsy's aunt. Her father is in the navy right now, and her mother—"

With a wave of her hand, Mrs. Peterson cut Aunt Gertrude off. "Oh, you don't have to tell me about her!"

My ears perked up, and my stomach fluttered. *My father? My mother?*

Mrs. Peterson reached down and stroked the top of my head. "Mrs. Betty Stroberg used to leave this poor child at the front door out in the cold without any supervision! I'd drive up and find her shivering and crying for her mommy. I'm very relieved to know that someone responsible is taking care of her now."

A flicker of memory flashed through my mind of me sitting outside the preschool doors, cold and sobbing.

My aunt looked uncomfortable. "Well, yes. *Our* side of the family is very reliable. I mean—"

Mrs. Peterson cut her off again, both women thoroughly embarrassed now. "Yes, of course. I didn't mean to imply. At any rate, I assume that you would like to enroll Patsy?"

My aunt nodded.

"Is she toilet trained yet?"

Aunt Gertrude shook her head, no.

"I'm sorry, but I told Mrs. Stroberg that her daughter could not return until she was potty-trained. We do not change diapers."

That's the day I found out I had a mother. Her name was Mrs. Stroberg. I was three years old.

Aunt Gertrude said, "Oh, Mrs. Peterson, I have just had a baby, and I need to have Patsy in school."

"I agree. Patsy is bright and should be in school." She smiled down at me. "You want to come to preschool, don't you, Patsy?"

I nodded emphatically.

Looking back at my aunt, she chuckled. "As I recall, Patsy is a bundle of energy. I suspect this would be good for both of you."

Aunt Gertrude smiled. "Indeed."

"But we have our rules. When Patsy is toilet trained, we will admit her." With that, Mrs. Peterson turned on her heels and disappeared back into her office. Case closed.

We walked home, and as soon as we got our coats off and Marilyn was napping in her crib, I was plopped down on the small toilet. "You must go in the potty rather than wear a diaper. I can't have two babies in diapers to care for. Now that Marilyn's here, it's time for you to grow up."

I nodded as if that made sense, although it didn't. Why couldn't I wear my diaper to preschool? What did Marilyn have to do with my growing up? Did she want me to grow taller? There was no explanation, but I wanted to make Aunt Gertrude happy. And I really wanted to go to school.

I nodded as if that made sense, although it didn't.

So, I did my best to follow all my aunt's instructions. I would sit at the table quietly and wait while Aunt Gertrude brought me a soft-boiled egg each morning. It was so pretty in its special egg cup. There was toast, too, and I liked toast.

"Here's how you take the shell off the top, Patsy."

"I know, I know! Let me do it, Aunt Gertrude!" I tapped ever so gently on the warm egg.

"Good. Now pick off the shell so there is room for your spoon." It was so exciting when I could finally eat my egg. I loved how Aunt Gertrude would sit across from me, feeding baby Marilyn. She had a big smile when I finally took my first bite.

When I finished my breakfast, Aunt Gertrude immediately put me on the potty. "Let me know when you go, Patsy. I'm going to change Marilyn's diaper now." I'd sit there listening to the birds outside and seeing the patterns in the tile floor. Sometimes I would sing. I really liked the echoes of the bathroom.

"I went poop!"

Before too long, I was officially potty-trained.

Each morning, Aunt Gertrude got me dressed, fixed my hair, and tucked Marilyn into her stroller. We'd walk down one block to the preschool, noticing the changing trees, flower-filled gardens, and the weather. I loved going to school with so many other children and the fun activities there—in fact, I loved everything about school except for the beets they forced me to eat each day. I genuinely detested eating lunch there. Beets.

I didn't like beets the first moment I saw them. I pushed the plate away. But this was 1943, and if someone put beets on your plate, you ate them. The childcare worker scolded me. "There are children starving in Europe! You eat what's put in front of you!"

So I dutifully ate them. At that moment, we all discovered that beets didn't like me any more than I liked them. Immediately beets came flying out of my mouth, spewing all over my dress, the plate, and the child sitting next to me. Everyone rushed around to clean up the mess.

The next day, beets were served as usual. I ate them. I threw them up. It took a few days for everyone to see that beets and I were not on good terms. After cleaning beets off the front of my dress and Aunt Gertrude complaining that it was impossible to get beet stains out of my clothing, I was given a special dispensation for their sake, not mine. No beets for Patsy! I was delighted. Once that was resolved, there wasn't anything I didn't enjoy about school.

I was a natural at it. I liked learning and flourished with my teacher, who didn't seem to tire from my questions. While I was hushed and told to be quieter at home, my energy was welcomed and challenged in the classroom. Pegged as a "helper," I would assist with any activity I was allowed. It became my job to set up the little cots for each of us at nap time. After they were set up, I fought sleeping as I didn't want to miss a thing. But I relished the quiet and safety I knew at school.

Blackouts in Ohio

"Patsy, keep those tokens on the table. We can't afford to lose any of them." Grandma Davis had brought her tokens over to share with Gramma Stroberg and Aunt Gertrude. We sat around the kitchen table while I played with them.

The stacks of wooden coins were houses in my imagination. I had created a little neighborhood on the kitchen table. Sometimes, I would spin them into tornados like Uncle Alvar had taught me to do with a penny. These were smooth and tasted different than the penny did. I sat crisscrossed on the red bench seat. I loved to cup as many as possible in each hand and then dump them into the bowl my dress made in my lap. Lost in my imagination, I was mixing my ingredients for fresh bread, just like a grown-up lady.

Aunt Gertrude observed me as I played. "She's having a growth spurt. I can tell her old shoes are hurting her. How many tokens do we need?"

"Patsy, let me have those for a minute to count them." Gramma Stroberg wiped her hands on her apron, scooped me up and off the bench, and dumped my make-believe bread dough on the table before I was happily in her lap.

We watched together as Aunt Gertrude slid the circles across one by one into her hand. Gramma started smoothing my hair, and I was so happy.

"Forty-two. We have forty-two now."

"We need forty-eight," Grandma Davis said.

"We also need to get flour and sugar. That will be eight tokens. Here you go, Patsy, you can play with them now." Back in my chair, I knelt at the table and started stacking once again.

"I wish Betty would contribute a few of her tokens. We could get Patsy the shoes now." Aunt Gertrude made a clicking noise when she was displeased.

Grandma Davis looked away with an embarrassed look on her face. I didn't know what was upsetting her, but I knew something was wrong. I got down from the table and held my hands up for Grandma Davis to hold me. She smiled and pulled me into her lap, grateful for the diversion.

My aunt seemed annoyed. "She shows no interest in the child at all."

"Gertrude!" That's all my Gramma Stroberg needed to say to bring the topic to a close.

My aunt sighed and changed the subject. "These rations! The baby. Patsy. Alvar. Al. Oh, for so many reasons, I wish this war would end."

Gramma nodded. "I know. I just think of Al on the ship and Alvar on the front in France, and it gives me perspective."

Grandma Davis joined back into the conversation. "If all goes as planned, Al should be on land for a five-week rotation soon."

Aunt Gertrude went into the kitchen and started putting away the clean dishes. "Oh, how I wish our guys were home safely right now! And I wish that we had enough tokens for Patsy's shoes."

"Stop fretting, Gertrude. I trust the good Lord will take care of us all." Gramma Stroberg said that often. "In two weeks, we will get more tokens and can choose Patsy's new shoes."

"We need to figure out her size," Aunt Gertrude said.

I kept playing with the tokens while sitting on Grandma Davis's lap. Gramma Stroberg continued to sew, and Aunt Gertrude started fixing dinner. I didn't understand the tension in the room, but I believed Gramma Stroberg's words that the good Lord would take care of all of us.

Gramma Stroberg picked up the newspaper on the table and began to read the updates on the war. Her face went white.

"What is it, Mom?" Aunt Gertrude asked.

Gramma Stroberg put down the paper. "They are calling for a regulation blackout starting tonight to 'make our city invisible to potential enemy planes.' The sirens will go off at nine."

"What?" Grandma Davis whispered. "They're afraid we'll actually get bombed? Like the air raids in London?"

My Gramma Stroberg nodded.

"Well, I'd better get home and get the blankets out right away. I'll need Roy's help to put them over the windows." Grandma Davis stood up abruptly.

"Yes, of course," my aunt said. "Once the sun sets, they'll patrol the streets to see if any light can be seen from our windows." She walked Grandma Davis to the door. I could see that the blackout drills scared them all. A sadness fell over me. I felt very small at that moment. And very alone.

That afternoon, my aunt and grandmother pulled blankets out of the closet and hung them from the windows. We were ready when the sun went down, and the siren blasted through the air. A blackout. "Mom, what if Cleveland is a target like Manchester or Liverpool?" Aunt Gertrude was obviously anxious and needed the comfort of her mother.

"Oh, Lord, keep us safe," she prayed out loud. "Now, let's all anchor these down so the house is good and dark. We are doing our part to make Ohio undetectable."

Oblivious to the fact that the country lived in fear that enemy forces might invade inland and bomb US cities, I saw it as a fun game of turning off the lights and living in the glow of candlelight. From time to time, air raid drills were called. Three long blasts of a siren, then a pause, repeated until there was an "all-clear" declared. No one seemed to know if the drills were for practicing or responding to a genuine threat.

As Marilyn got older, Aunt Gertrude bathed us together in the tub. I helped my aunt by playing with the cups and bowls in the warm suds with Marilyn. I was, after all, a big girl now. Wanting to please my aunt and Gramma Stroberg, I took responsibility for Marilyn very seriously.

On the nights we had blackouts, the shimmering, shifting light made the warm bathroom seem all the warmer. I felt safe and content.

I especially enjoyed the short time I had the bath all to myself once Aunt Gertrude took Marilyn out first to get her ready for bed. I slid up and down the side of the bathtub, always careful not to splash any water out on the floor. I knew that big girls never splash water on the floor.

I Have a Father?

Gramma Stroberg and I shared one of the two bedrooms in the house, accessed by a steep set of stairs. When I was around four and a half, I realized that Gramma was looking older and thinner. I heard people whisper about "cancer," and I could see from her face that she was often in pain.

The doctor came every few days to visit and give her medicine, but it didn't seem to help much. It was hard to watch her suffer. By the time I was five, Gramma Stroberg stopped wearing her apron and didn't cook anymore. Soon, she never left the bed. Our room took on a rather dank, sickly smell that unsettled my stomach.

One afternoon, when Marilyn was nearly two, she and I were playing in the living room. Aunt Gertrude was making tea to take up to the doctor visiting Gramma. We heard a knock on the door.

My Aunt went to the door and opened it. "Al! You're here!" she cried out.

I'd heard about this man named Al, not that anyone told me about him. They just mentioned him now and then. So I was curious to see who he was. Al was dressed in his navy whites. He took off his sailor hat and walked into the room, giving Aunt Gertrude a stiff hug.

"I wouldn't let anyone stop me," he said firmly.

"Of course," she nodded. "I'm so glad you got here in time."

I looked up at this tall and thin stranger. He looked down at me and scooped me up in his arms. He smelled of cigarette smoke and Old Spice. "Patsy!" He held me so tight it scared me. *Who is this man?*

Aunt Gertrude solved the mystery. "Patsy, your daddy is home!"

My daddy? Awkward and uncertain, I stiffened in his embrace.

Aunt Gertrude smiled at me in his arms. "Patsy, this is your father. Remember, he's been on a big ship, fighting in the war." She ruffled my hair and nodded that it was all okay, and I relaxed.

Like a found piece of a puzzle, I realized Al was my father. My daddy. I had always wanted a father. Now, I willingly hugged him.

She smiled but had a worried tone. "Al, I thought you were at a special training program."

"Oh, I have been. But I needed to see Mom."

"She's upstairs. She is so frail. You should go see her now."

Daddy put me on his hip and carried me upstairs to Gramma's bedside. He sat down, placing me on his lap. He stared at his mother's face; her eyes closed.

The doctor was there. Aunt Gertrude stood in the corner as if trying to hide from what she saw. The doctor leaned down and held the stethoscope to her chest. He looked up with a sad face. "She is still with us, but she's in a coma. She won't wake up." Turning to my dad, he said, "I'm glad you made it here, Al, but I'm sorry you missed the chance to talk with her."

A deep sadness fell over my father's face. I sat in his lap as he sat near her bed. I looked at Gramma, then up at him and over to Aunt Gertrude. "Is Gramma going to die?"

Before anyone could respond, Gramma sighed. We all stared at her. She opened her eyes and looked directly at my father. "Al, take good care of Patsy." She closed her eyes again. We stayed there by her side, watching her sleep. Sorrow hung in the room, but something was new in me. Gramma, Daddy, and I were connected. I belonged.

"Al, take good care of Patsy," were the last words she ever spoke, and they were about caring for me. She woke up for me! This memory is one I have cherished all my life, feeling the love from my Gramma and meeting my father.

I was sent to Aunt Gertrude and Uncle Alvar's room to play with Marilyn for the rest of the day. That night, Dad slept on the couch, and I was allowed, for the first time, to sleep in my aunt's and uncle's bedroom. They made a little bed on the floor out of blankets since I was too big to share Marilyn's crib.

> "Al, take good care of Patsy," were the last words she ever spoke, and they were about caring for me.

I peered into my room across the hall when I woke up the following day. Her bed was empty. Gramma was gone.

I heard talking downstairs and found Aunt Gertrude and my dad sitting at the table; he had his head in his hands. I crawled up onto his lap, but he didn't seem to notice.

Aunt Gertrude was obviously distressed. "What do you mean you didn't get permission to come home?"

My dad shrugged. "After all I've done for this country, there was no way I was going to let them keep me from seeing Mom one last time."

They sat in silence. Dad mumbled, "This war."

Aunt Gertrude was still in shock. "You're saying you are AWOL?"

I slid off Dad's lap and sat on the red bench with my doll. I thought about where Gramma was now.

My dad grimaced. "It's not technically AWOL, Gertrude. Don't be so overly dramatic."

"So what happens when someone leaves the base but it's not tech-ni-cal-ly A-WOL?" She seemed to be trying to annoy him as she emphasized each syllable. "What is going to happen to you? Are they going to come here and arrest you? That's all we need. Mother dying, and you carted off to jail."

"I just left the base for a few days, that's all. Caught the train and made it just in time. It's not a big deal. Gertrude, I had to see her."

Aunt Gertrude nodded. "Yes, of course. I understand. But Al—"

"I had to see her before …" My father's eyes filled with tears.

Aunt Gertrude put her hand on her brother's arm. Neither of them spoke for a few minutes until Dad broke the silence. "But I have to get back to the base as soon as possible."

Aunt Gertrude sighed. "You'll have to miss the funeral?"

Dad's shoulders dropped.

"Of course, you must get back. Of course." She paused as she looked into his eyes. "But will they let you back on base?"

Dad got up, left for a minute, rifled through his bag, and walked back into the room with two large bottles of rum. I stared at them, wondering what made them special.

"Look what I picked up at one of the train stations. Somewhere, there will be a guard who will gladly let me back in without any trouble."

"Oh, good Lord!" My aunt gasped and shook her head slowly.

"The sooner I'm back, the less likely I'll be missed."

"Well, we will miss you here. Let me pack you something to eat," Aunt Gertrude said, getting up from the table.

My dad nodded. He reached over and lifted me back onto his lap. He held me close. "Oh, my dear Patsy." I knew I belonged with him. He was my daddy. I liked him and wanted him to stay. It seemed like time stood still, yet it went by in a flash.

Aunt Gertrude brought a wrapped package of food from the kitchen and put it into his duffle bag with the two bottles of rum.

My dad kissed me lightly on the cheek. "Daddy will come home to stay very soon, Patsy. Don't worry." His eyes filled with tears again. I held onto him and felt an ache inside. He kissed me once again, this time on my head. Upon hearing the taxicab pull up, he stood and inhaled deeply as he straightened his back. He looked around the kitchen, soaking in our attentive glances and his family home. With a turn, he was gone.

I cried hard. I cried so hard that Aunt Gertrude walked me up to my room.

"Calm down, Patsy, and remember, don't tell anyone that your father was here." She ushered me into my room. "Stay here until Marilyn wakes up." She closed the door behind her.

I buried my head in the pillow to suffocate my sobs. For the first time, I was in that room by myself. In one day's time, I found my father, then lost both him and my Gramma. I cried myself to sleep, missing her and wondering when I would see him again.

We're Going to Be a Family

We never spoke about my father's brief appearance when Gramma died. Life went on as it had.

Sometimes, Grandma Davis and Grandpa Roy visited to listen to the radio announcements. Our radio was a rather large contraption that sat on top of a cabinet in the living room. It was a dark gray, rectangular metal box with one large, white gauge on the front near the top in the middle. It had numbers on it and a tiny red metal arrow that moved when you searched for a station. Below it was a round dial with numerals—you could turn it left or right. Below that were four other little toggle switches. A squared piece of fine-meshed metal was on the right of the dial. The sound came out of it. My family would gather around the radio whenever something big happened, or sometimes, to dance to music.

The grown-ups sat very still as they strained to hear a raspy voice coming through the radio static. Marilyn and I had to be quiet. The responsibility to keep her still fell onto my shoulders. Not only were we forbidden to talk, but we also couldn't fidget or get fussy, or someone would send us to our room.

Most of the time, my relatives' faces were sad, strained, or tearful. I didn't like having to sit still and watch the grown-ups look so scared. I couldn't follow the man's voice with his big words—victory, troops, casualties, V-day, Allies—and none of it made sense to me.

As a five-year-old, I understood that Americans were fighting in two places even though I had no understanding of where those places might be—in Europe against the Nazis and in the Pacific against the Japanese. We'd won in Europe, so it wasn't too long until Uncle Alvar came home.

Everyone was elated when he first walked in the door, but it didn't take long for me to pick up on the fact that Aunt Gertrude was troubled.

"Patsy, you and Marilyn need to play quietly. You know how the noise irritates Uncle Alvar." I nodded because I heard him sigh and startle in his chair when we got loud, but I didn't understand why.

He was always smoking, and he didn't tease Aunt Gertrude like he used to. I heard Aunt Gertrude and him talking one night when I was supposed to be sleeping.

"Alvar, I miss you. I miss your hugs."

"Gert, leave me be. I am going to sleep."

I could hear her crying for a time before I fell into a troubled sleep.

Many nights, Aunt Gertrude sat alone in the small living room crouched over her sewing, just like when my uncle was gone.

My daddy was in the other war, the one in the Pacific. He was on a ship in the middle of the battle. The worry in our home was thick in the air.

One day, a man came to the door and delivered a telegram. Uncle Alvar read it out loud to Aunt Gertrude. "US Navy reports to the family of Seaman Al Stroberg. He is severely wounded at sea." We learned that when a kamikaze plane hit the ship he was on, the impact threw him onto the bulkhead. It broke his back, and he was in transit to a military hospital called Walter Reed. Overwhelmed with the news, Aunt Gertrude nearly collapsed onto a nearby chair.

I ran to her, and she held me tight.

"Will Daddy be okay?" I cried out.

Uncle Alvar spoke first, probably intending to comfort his wife rather than answer my question. "Yes, don't worry. He's getting the best care in the world right here in America. They are taking very good care of him."

Not long after we got the telegram, the Japanese surrendered.

"The war is over!" Grandma Davis said. She had come over. And I'd never seen Aunt Gertrude so excited. She started crying, Grandma jumped up, and the two grabbed each other's hands. They were so happy. They had tears running down their faces. Grandpa Roy smiled, and even Uncle Alvar seemed relieved and more comfortable. In a rare moment of solidarity, the two men shook hands and patted each other on the back.

Aunt Gertrude knelt down on the floor and looked at Marilyn and me. "Girls, sweet girls, the war is over!" She welcomed us into her arms.

"The good Lord *has* taken care of us," I said.

"My goodness!" Aunt Gertrude exclaimed. "From the mouth of babes!"

Grandma Davis sat in a nearby chair and beckoned for me to come into her arms. She hugged me and then looked me in the eyes. "Do you know what this means, Patsy?"

I shook my head no.

"As soon as your daddy gets better, he's coming home."

"For another visit?"

"No, Patsy. For good!"

I'd hoped to see my daddy for Christmas, but it wasn't until early Spring of 1946 that he arrived. Aunt Gertrude called me down from where Marilyn and I were playing in our room. "Patsy! Look! It's your daddy."

I ran down the stairs and then stopped in my tracks. When I met my father the day my Gramma Stroberg died, he was in his Navy whites, and he had scooped me up and hugged me. Now, he stood looming over me in khakis and a flannel shirt, his body stiff and his face stern—no trace of a smile. He touched the top of my head and said my name, but even his voice sounded different.

"Al, sit down here. What can I get you?" Aunt Gertrude was fussing with a pillow and a cup of coffee. I studied him, trying to recognize his face. He had a metal collar poking out of his shirt, and his chin rested on a pad.

Uncle Alvar offered Dad a cigarette. He took it, and when Uncle Alvar held a lit match toward him, Dad leaned forward with his entire body. He didn't bend in the middle. He took a deep drag and looked at all of us as he blew out the foul-smelling smoke. "They sent me back to the mainland three months ago."

"Uh-huh, well, glad you didn't get shot up, Al," my uncle said. "But how is your back?"

"It's healing," Dad said. He stared blindly forward.

"You've been ten weeks at Walter Reed in Bethesda, right?"

"Uh-hmmm."

"That's a long time in a hospital."

Before my dad responded, he sighed and squinted his eyes a little. Holding his cigarette in one hand and coffee cup in the other, he said, "Yeah. I don't remember some details." Dad stopped, sipping the steaming liquid. "They told us that the kamikazes were coming. We looked up, but the sky was empty. I heard them before I saw them. The buzzing got louder and louder. And then I saw one heading right toward us." He paused. "But that blast!" He made a swooshing noise that made the steam from his cup disappear. "There was a deafening crash and a blinding flash of light. I bounced on top of a pipe, and something threw me into the bulkhead. Then it all went black. I don't remember much after that."

"Al, you're so brave." Aunt Gertrude sat on the couch across from the men in the chairs now. She held Marilyn, and I leaned back, touching her legs. "I'm so grateful that you're here now, and Patsy has her dad back. The war is over."

"That's right, Gertrude. We are glad you are back, Al." Uncle Alvar cleared his throat and rubbed the arm of the chair.

Dad finally looked up to meet their eyes. "I have to wear this!" He thumped his chest, and it sounded like he banged on a box. "I'll be in a brace for about a year." He shook his head and grimaced.

"Oh, Al, I can see you're in pain," my aunt said. She sounded very concerned and sad.

"That part under your chin is connected?" Uncle Alvar always wanted to know how things worked. Me too.

"Yeah. The brace goes from my chin to my hips."

Aunt Gertrude's tears brimmed in her eyes. "I know Mom would be proud of you. Let me get you some more coffee. Alvar, how is your cup?"

Before Aunt Gertrude could stand up, my dad blurted out, "Where's Betty? I thought..."

My ears perked up. I wanted to know about this woman named Betty. What did she have to do with me and my dad? The grown-ups looked at each other but said nothing. Aunt Gertrude put Marilyn on a blanket on the floor and tapped my shoulder to move over so she could stand up. She took my dad's cup while he forcefully snuffed out his cigarette in the ashtray. She walked out of the room without a word.

Uncle Alvar looked at her with envy and took a deep breath. "Al, we told Betty's parents you were coming back today. They'll be here."

"Is Betty coming with them, Alvar?"

"I don't know. We don't see much of Betty. You know how she is. All or nothing."

Aunt Gertrude walked back in with two cups of hot coffee and set them in front of the men. "I'm sorry to be the one to have to say this, Al, but Alvar is right. She's like a light bulb—switched on at full brightness or off in total darkness. She's gone dark most of the time you've been gone."

Uncle Alvar jumped in. "Now, Mrs. Davis comes over to see Patsy all the time. She's a good grandmother. But we, well, uh, we rarely see Betty." Marilyn and I were playing together with the blocks stored under the coffee table, but I kept my ears focused on the conversation. I felt the tension of the grown-ups' words, but I didn't understand it at all.

"According to the neighbors renting your side of the duplex, she comes by once a month to pick up rent," Aunt Gertrude said.

"It's right next door. You mean Betty doesn't even stop in?" Dad banged the bottom of his red and white cigarette pack and shook out another one. He groaned while he struck a match and lit it.

"Al, she never tells us when she's coming for the rent. She shows no interest in Patsy." The little house I'd made with Marilyn collapsed with the last block I'd placed. The grown-ups didn't even notice.

I looked over at Dad. His face had changed, and he shook a bit like he was yelling inside his head.

Aunt Gertrude used her head to direct attention to me. "Little ears are tuning in. But let me say that you know Betty's family.

Betty is very good at being invisible when things are difficult.

The drinking, the arguments—it's been hard for everyone during the war, but especially difficult for them financially. Betty is very good at being invisible when things are difficult."

Looking back, I believe it was at that moment Dad realized that his wife had abandoned his child to the sole care of his sister and brother-in-law. "I knew Patsy was staying here with you, of course. But you're saying she doesn't even come to see her?"

Aunt Gertrude shook her head. "Patsy doesn't even know her, Al. Have you been in touch with her?"

He looked defeated. "I rarely got a letter, and then it was vague about Betty's situation."

Aunt Gertrude made a feeble defense on Betty's behalf. "You know she fell into a deep depression after Patsy was born."

My dad said nothing. Uncle Alvar filled the silence. "That's enough talk about her. It's clear to me that you need some more rest right now, Al. You stay with us, and we'll figure out how to change things. I'm just so glad you're home."

My dad rubbed his eyes, and I thought he was going to cry. But when he put his hand down, his eyes flashed hot, and his voice was stern. He was not going to let anything divert him from this conversation. Like a deflating tire, he hissed. "I want those renters out of my house *today!*"

His eyes met mine as if seeing me for the first time. "Come over here, Patsy." I bravely crawled out from under the coffee table. He pulled me into his lap. With the rigid metal brace between us and his severe tone, he didn't feel soft and warm like before. But his fingers stroked my hair sweetly.

He made a declaration. "Betty *is* coming back where she belongs. I'll see to that. We are going to be a family again."

You're Not the Mommy I Want

Dad slept on the couch for a few weeks while the family renting our side of the duplex packed and moved. Aunt Gertrude doted on him, knowing his body was in pain. Like her husband, her brother was different after the war. The vigilance and danger had taken their toll. Marilyn and I learned to play very quietly if the men were resting.

The other duplex had previously been rented furnished, so while Grandma Davis and Aunt Gertrude dove in to wash and scrub every inch of the vacated unit, the men checked out the furniture and mended any pieces that had been broken or where the screws had come loose. Within a few short days, the house was ready for us.

Aunt Gertrude and Grandma Davis walked upstairs and told me to follow them. "Now, Patsy, we must pack up your things."

"Why?" I asked.

"Because you're going to move next door with your parents—"

"My parents?" Surprised and excited, I also didn't understand. In all the cleaning and commotion, no one had thought to explain to me what was happening. No one.

The women looked at each other, stunned that I had been left in the dark.

"Yes, Patsy," my aunt said. "You, your dad, and your mom are moving in next door. You're going to be a family."

Excitement filled my heart! In my five-year-old mind, I'd dreamed of this day. I wanted a mom and a dad like the kids at school and Marilyn had. *What will my mom look like? What will she say? Will she like me? Will I like her?* My thoughts were all over the place with one question after another, and I jumped around dancing with anticipation. Marilyn followed my example.

"Settle down, girls," Grandma Davis said. "We need to pack up your clothes and toys."

In all the cleaning and commotion, no one had thought to explain to me what was happening. No one.

Marilyn and I happily joined in, opening drawers and folding my belongings. I was too excited to realize that I was about to leave the only home I'd known.

We had just filled the last box when Uncle Alvar called up the stairs. "They're here."

I dashed down the stairs and out the front door. Suddenly feeling uncomfortable, I took two steps back into the doorway. Grandma and Aunt Gertrude, with Marilyn on her hip, joined me. My dad opened the car door for a pretty, dark-haired woman with lots of lipstick. I was frozen, unsure of what to do. Grandma Davis sweetly took my hand and walked me down the few stairs to the driveway.

"Patsy, this is your mother."

I'd wanted a mother for so long, but now I wasn't sure. I looked back at Aunt Gertrude in the frame of the front door. Grandma guided my hand out toward my mother's. "Betty, say hello to Patsy."

It came as a cruel blow when I connected the dots. The unseen, distant lady, Betty, was my mother, and she was here. She looked down at me, seeming as unsure as I felt. Grandma pushed our hands together. I grabbed her fingers that lay limp in my little hand. She pulled away and patted me on the head. "Patsy, what a big girl you've become." A small smile played at the edges of her mouth. "And so pretty."

I grinned at the compliment, longing for her to scoop me into her arms and smother me with kisses. But she glanced over at my father as if asking him to rescue her. Dad said, "Let's go see our duplex. It's certainly cleaned up."

"Don't just stand there, Roy," Grandma Davis said. "Get your daughter's suitcases out of the car." Grandpa Roy jumped toward the car, startled that anyone expected him to participate. Dad put his hand on the small of my mother's back and softly guided her toward the house and onto the porch.

"Alvar, the last of Patsy's items are boxed upstairs. Could you bring them over here too?" Grandma Davis asked.

My uncle was grateful for a task to keep him away from conversation. "Sure thing, Mrs. Davis."

Aunt Gertrude, with Marilyn still in her arms, chose to linger back. "You get settled in. I'll have supper for everyone here at five-thirty, okay?"

My dad looked at my mom, then at his sister, aware of her kindness and grace. "Thanks, Gertrude."

We walked through our front door, each carrying our dreams and fears.

Grandma Davis helped me make my bed and put my clothes in the small dresser. My dresses and coat were in the closet. The room was the mirror opposite of my room in Aunt Gertrude's side of the duplex.

> *We walked through our front door, each carrying our dreams and fears.*

I was in the bathroom when I heard them talking in the hall. "I'm not going to supper, Al."

"Betty, please. After all that's gone on?"

Grandma went into the hall. "Betty! You have to go. At least pretend to be grateful that Gertrude has raised your child for the past two years!"

My mother was livid, her face streaming with hot tears. "So that's how it's going to be? You throwing my suffering in my face?" Though upstairs, I could still hear everything. My stomach hurt, and I felt like crying. I was scared. I didn't know why they were fighting.

Dad jumped in. "No, Betty. No one wants to throw anything in your face. It's a new start. No looking back."

Grandma made a quick change in strategy. "Oh, yes, Betty. I didn't mean that. I really didn't. This is supposed to be a happy occasion. Even Evelyn and Bill are coming to join us. This move will be a wonderful new start for everyone."

Mom was horrified. "My sister will be here? What could be worse than having her gloat over me? Are you all trying to torture me? Mother, no! Tell them I have a headache." She stormed into the bedroom and slammed the door. I jumped at the noise and felt the vibration throughout my body.

Dad slumped against the wall with a hard thump as his brace hit the plaster. I wasn't used to Dad being upset.

Grandma Davis left my room and stomped down the stairs, running into an angry Grandpa Roy. "You do know that everyone can hear you, right? The walls of this duplex are paper thin!"

"How humiliating," Grandma Davis cried.

Dad slowly made it down the stairs, one step at a time. I followed, aware that his back was hurting him. A woman I didn't know poked her head inside the duplex door. "Well, hello there! Bill and I are here. Is the party here or next door?"

"Oh, Evelyn!" Grandma Davis covered her face and cried. "Your little sister is making a horrible scene, refusing to go to dinner and after all that Gertrude has done for Betty."

Evelyn nodded to my dad. "Hello, Al, good to see you back from the war." Seeing me spy from behind my dad's legs, she said, "Well, you must be Patsy!"

I nodded, and she introduced herself. "I'm your Aunt Evelyn. Your mother's older sister."

A strange, tall man walked in. "What's going on over here? There's a table full of food next door waiting for us. Gertrude and Alvar are just sitting there wondering what the holdup is, not that it's much of a secret with all the yelling."

Aunt Evelyn sneered at her husband. "Oh, Bill, you know Betty. Always causing a scene."

Grandma Davis was beside herself. "Oh, I can't face Gertrude. We are heading back to the trailer *now*!" With that, my grandparents left the house, followed by Aunt Evelyn and Uncle Bill, who I assumed was her husband. They got into their cars and drove off without a word to my aunt and uncle next door.

Obviously saddened, my dad crossed the porch to his sister's home. I heard muffled conversation from inside. Dad reappeared holding a casserole dish, with Aunt Gertrude following behind, carrying vegetables and biscuits. Marilyn brought up the rear with a cake. She shrugged her shoulders at me, and I nodded my head. I wished I could go back over to the room I shared with Marilyn rather than have to stay with my confusing mom.

Aunt Gertrude and Marilyn went back to their duplex, and Dad served himself and me some of the casserole and biscuits. We ate in silence in the kitchen. When we were done, I asked, "What about Mom? Won't she be hungry?"

He shook his head. "Go on and get ready for bed."

I put on my nightgown and brushed my teeth while Dad sat in the kitchen smoking. I came back down, into the kitchen.

"Dad, will you tuck me in?"

Startled by my question, he finished his cigarette and walked behind me to my room. He didn't say prayers the way Aunt Gertrude always did. Because of his brace, he couldn't bend over to kiss me goodnight. He pulled my blanket up to my chest and tousled my hair. "Good night, honey." He walked to the door and then paused and turned toward me.

"It will get better, Pasty." I could see that he was trying to assure me. "Once she gets settled in. You'll see."

I pulled the blanket over my head. "No one ever tells me anything! Why do I have to live here instead of with Aunt Gertrude?"

He said nothing. I peered out from under the covers and saw an empty doorway. He'd already gone without hearing a word I'd said.

Sunday, the One Day of Joy

The next morning, I was up early. I snuck out the front door and knocked on Aunt Gertrude's back door. She came to the door a bit groggy and let me in. I ran into Marilyn's room and snuggled into her warm bed with her. Once everyone woke up, Aunt Gertrude fed us breakfast, and Marilyn and I played together.

I did this every morning until the day Aunt Gertrude opened the duplex door with a frown on her face. She said, "I'm sorry, Patsy, but Uncle Alvar doesn't like you waking us up so early. You have to stop coming over in the morning like this."

"I promise I'll be good, Aunt Gertrude. Please, please let me come in." Tears flowed down my cheeks.

"I'm sorry, Patsy. I am. But this has to stop."

"No, I promise. I will be quiet as a mouse. I won't—"

My pleas were cut short as she closed the door. I turned around and went back into my house, my heart broken.

My mom was a stranger to me and didn't seem to like me very much. She was always terribly sad and slept all day, getting up only to fix dinner for my father and pretend everything was fine. I didn't see my dad often because he now worked twelve hours daily at the gas station. I was asleep when he left in the morning, and by the time he got home and we ate dinner, it was my bedtime. My mom didn't want to get up to take me to school, and Aunt Gertrude didn't want to intrude, so I played alone all day.

The loneliness was dispelled one day a week—on Sunday. Like most good Swedes in our neighborhood, I was raised Lutheran and loved going to church with Aunt Gertrude and Marilyn. Every Sunday morning, I'd show up next door at eight-thirty, wanting to get ready for church.

"Here's your dress, Patsy. I ironed it for you."

"Thanks, Aunt Gertrude."

"Once you have it on, come back over here, and I'll fix your hair. I'm almost finished with Marilyn's."

Marilyn and I rode in the backseat together. During the week, I was a bit jealous of Marilyn, but on Sunday, I could pretend that I still lived with them. She and I rolled down the windows so that it would make it hard to hear each other. We giggled all the way to church, and as we tried to guess what the other was saying, we would get silly.

The loneliness was dispelled one day a week— on Sunday.

Once we arrived at St. John's Lutheran Church, Marilyn and I followed Aunt Gertrude like little ducklings through the big doors. Since I was older, I sometimes held Marilyn's hand because she felt shy or wanted to run off. Inside, we would walk down the stairs to the children's church. Since Marilyn and I were three years apart, Aunt Gertrude first walked Marilyn to her classroom with the younger kids and then took me to join the older children. Aunt Gertrude would then go back upstairs for the church service. The kids' program had grown-ups sharing Bible stories and asking questions. I liked it when we sang. I felt the music in my body. We sang my favorite song at the end of every Sunday School class.

Jesus loves me this I know, for the Bible tells me so.
Little ones to Him belong. They are weak, but He is strong.
Yes, Jesus loves me. Yes, Jesus loves me.
Yes, Jesus loves me. The Bible tells me so.

I knew the words to this song, and I'd sing so loudly. Mrs. Kelly, the youth pastor, would always put her hand on my shoulder and stroke my hair as I sang to God.

It was then, as a young child, that I began my spiritual journey. There was a clear identity on my father's side of the family. We were Swedes. We were Lutherans. Both were, more or less, the same thing. And the good Lord, like Gramma always said, had taken care of us through the war.

In contrast, my mother's side of the family was Irish Catholic. But that had no impact on me. My mom and the rest of her family weren't church-goers. Nearly everyone in our neighborhood went to the Lutheran church except my dad, always working at his gas station, and my mother, always in bed.

As summer approached, there was a joy that swept almost everyone up. The summer of 1946, after the war ended, brought one of my best childhood memories. I still remember the perfumed air of Cleveland, where lilac bushes thrived all over town. It was a moment of being happy and just being a kid.

Family gatherings had been few and far between, having grown up under the oppression of the war, financial instability, and emotional circumstances. However, after the war, every Tuesday, some of my mother's side of the family, the Irish, met at Metropolitan Park. Grandma Davis had twelve brothers and sisters, plus their husbands, wives, and children. They made a massive crowd. But on the Fourth of July, both sides of the family quickly reconnected at the park. We were so overjoyed to be Americans and to be in peacetime.

I was delighted to spend time with my closest cousins, Janny, Aunt Evelyn's daughter from my mom's side of the family, and Marilyn from my dad's side. We spent the whole day together. And it wasn't just our families. It seemed like everyone in town showed up at Metropolitan Park for the Fourth of July parade. After the parade, we threw our blankets down on the freshly cut grass and gathered for a picnic.

There was an abundance of food, including my favorite sugar cookies. Some of my aunts played Penny Ante poker and even taught me! I ran from one friendly face to another.

My dad usually worked seven days a week at the gas station, but took some time off to celebrate the Fourth of July. And my mom even showed up. All little girls think their mothers are beautiful, but the older I got, the more I realized my mother was stunningly gorgeous. It was the first time since we moved in together that my parents looked joyful together.

The sky was brilliant, and the trees were full with their summer splendor. The afternoon sun warmed my back and the top of my head as I played by myself for a time in the sandbox. It was a calm and peaceful day. *I am so happy!* I sifted and smoothed my piles of grayish-tan sand. I wanted to feel happy like this for the rest of my life. It was and is a memory I cherish. That moment was engraved in my soul. I felt safe, loved, and full of joy.

Cocoa and Toast

Come fall of 1946, I started the first grade. I got myself up each morning, picked out my clothes, and walked to school on my own. Every day when I got home from school, I went into my parents' bedroom and asked my mother for a snack. Groggy, she would drag herself into the kitchen, but I knew she was annoyed with me. Some days, she just kept sleeping.

One afternoon, when I got home, she led me to the kitchen and said, "You're six years old now, Patsy. You can make your own food." She got a small saucepan out of the cabinet and told me to get the milk out of the refrigerator as she reached up in the cupboard and got out the sugar bowl and a tin of cocoa. I was excited that my mother was teaching me something. I didn't want to make any mistakes. Carefully, I handed her the glass milk container.

> *You're six years old now, Patsy. You can make your own food.*

She turned the dial for the front gas burner and said, "Look here, Patsy. See how low the flame is? Always keep it very low, or you'll burn the milk."

I nodded.

"And I should hope you will be very careful with the fire. Don't want the house to burn down."

I was nervous. No one had ever let me touch the stove before.

"Get a teacup and pour the milk into it to measure the right amount." She showed me and poured the milk into the heated pan. It sizzled slightly.

"Always keep stirring so it doesn't scald. Then measure out two teaspoons of cocoa and one teaspoon of sugar." She waited for a moment and then said, "Well, go ahead, Patsy!"

"Oh, okay." I rushed to get a spoon and measured out the cocoa and sugar while my mother kept stirring.

"Once it's dissolved, take the pan over to the sink and pour the cocoa into the cup." She demonstrated, and there was a perfectly wonderful cup of cocoa.

"Now, I want to show you how to make toast. You can do that while the cocoa is cooling off." That made sense to my six-year-old mind. "Get me a slice of bread."

I pulled the bread from the breadbox and handed her a slice. She popped it into the toaster and pulled down the lever. "You'll want some butter, Patsy."

I went back to the refrigerator and brought out the butter. Before long, the toast popped up from the toaster, and Mom showed me how to spread the butter without breaking the bread. "Get yourself a little plate and put the toast on it."

I was such a big girl! Getting my plate, I put the toast on it.

"Here's your cocoa, Patsy."

"Okay, okay, okay, Mom."

I couldn't believe that I was getting so much attention from her.

My mother spun on her heels and said, "Now, don't bother me anymore. You can take care of yourself."

And so, I did. I made myself cocoa and toast for breakfast, lunch, and snacks every day.

Mom managed to get herself out of bed by late afternoon, got dressed, and made dinner by the time my dad got home. He assumed my mother was feeding me breakfast, sending me to school with a sack lunch, and making snacks for me in the afternoon. But it wasn't long before he discovered the truth when my schoolteacher unintentionally intervened.

"Stop fidgeting with your hands," Mrs. Monroe told me as she passed by my desk.

I looked down and realized I was rubbing a wart on my right hand. "I've never had one of these before," I mused.

"It's a wart," she said as if saying a dirty word. I hid my hand; I was so embarrassed.

But in a few days, my wart situation got worse. Much worse. Another wart appeared, and then another and another. Within weeks, my entire right hand and arm, up to my shoulder, were covered with dozens of warts. I wore long-sleeved shirts to cover it, even when the weather was hot.

The sight of my warts repulsed my mother, so she took me to the doctor to have them removed. I had to get poked and have a blood test, which I hated, before meeting with the doctor. He examined my arm and hand with a frown on his face. "We may have to burn all of these off. Hmm, so many."

I pulled my arm away. "No, no burning."

He nodded. "It would not be pleasant with so many warts." He looked down at the papers in his hand. "Well, the blood test says you are anemic, so let's start with that problem first. Patricia, what do you usually eat for breakfast?"

"Cocoa and toast."

"And for lunch?"

"Cocoa and toast."

"Dinner?"

My mother became offended. "I cook a good dinner."

"She does," I said, defending my mother. "She gets out of bed to cook us dinner."

The doctor looked at her in disapproval. "Your sleeping habits are your business, but your daughter is anemic, and it appears to be because she eats primarily cocoa and toast. That's not sufficient for a growing young girl. She is malnourished."

He paused as if to let his words sink in. "So, from now on, feed your daughter Cheerios for breakfast and fix her a good lunch. I'll give you a prescription for strong vitamins. Please come back in one month."

I don't remember if we ever returned to that doctor, but I do remember eating lots of Cheerios and taking vitamins. Like a miracle, the warts on my hands and arms disappeared! Soon, I could wear short sleeves, no longer feeling like I needed to hide.

Why Don't You Believe Me?

My mother's emotions swung from one extreme to the other. There was no middle ground for her. When she wasn't in bed overcome with depression, she was lively and outgoing, often the life of the party. But that didn't mean that I enjoyed being around her. At the moments she was the most animated, she could erupt into a rage. I learned to walk on eggshells when she was happy. I never knew what would set my mother off.

By the time I was in the third grade, I realized I wasn't the only one who felt anxious when my mother got out of bed and joined in with the rest of us. Everyone, including my father, seemed intimidated by her stuffed feelings. This was made clear to me the summer my mom, Grandma Davis, Grandpa Roy, and I visited Grandma Davis's brother, Uncle Earl. There were neighbor girls to play with—Carol, who lived next door, and Linda, who lived a few houses away. They were eight years old, like me.

One Sunday, Carol and her family were gone for a while. "Mom, I'm bored. I wish Carol were home."

"Why don't you head over to her house and sit on their porch swing? They should be getting home anytime now." Happy to be outside, I bounded out the kitchen door to sit on their large porch and wait for them.

Linda saw me from her yard and joined me. "My Mom said Carol should be home soon. Let's sit and swing together."

The porch swing was old and creaked as we rocked it back and forth. The stuffing of the faded flowery cushion was peeking out. Linda was fidgeting with it.

"Don't pick at that, Linda." I watched her pull it out anyway and throw it on the ground. I picked it up and sat back down on the swing. She pulled out more, and she laughed.

"Stop doing that!" I was so mad. I knew it was wrong. Linda kept pulling it out of the hole, and I would push it back in.

I was collecting the white fluff from the ground as Carol and her folks drove up. I was holding two handfuls of stuffing. Immediately, Carol's mother jumped out of the car and started yelling at me. "Patsy Stroberg! What are you doing to our cushion, young lady?" Linda ran right away to her house.

I held up the stuffing. "Carol, see. I'm putting it back in!" They wouldn't listen as they clomped up their stairs toward me. "I told Linda to stop!"

Her mother made a clicking sound with her tongue while she shook her head. Even Carol yelled at me, "Patsy, why are you ruining our swing?"

"I was doing the right thing!" I ran home crying, went straight to my bedroom, and hid in a ball between the bed and the wall. I remember sobbing so hard. "I was doing the right thing. No one even listened to me! If Dad were here, he would listen."

Mom answered the front door, and I could hear their accusations through the wall. Carol and her mother told a story about me that wasn't true. "Patsy was there with the stuffing in her hand, Betty! I couldn't believe my eyes!"

I shuddered when I heard Mom's stern voice. "Patsy, come here."

I tried to speak, looking at my mom to help me. "I was putting the stuffing back in that Linda took out!" They all stared at me, and I knew my face was red. My stomach ached.

"I rescued the white fluff Linda picked out!"

My mother didn't believe me. "Patsy, manners, please. Watch your tone of voice."

"I was only putting the stuffing back in. She did it. Linda was the one who pulled it out." No one would listen to me.

Carol and her mother left, and my mother was furious. "You are so difficult, Patsy. A terrible little girl and a liar!" She spanked me, and I felt utterly betrayed. I hated my life. *I do my best to be a good girl, so why won't anyone believe me?*

Two days later, Mom was still angry with me. I stayed inside and played by myself. Fortunately, I had some books to read. That helped me get away from how lonely and mad I felt. I didn't want to talk to Carol or Linda, anyway. It was so unfair that my mother spanked me. I wanted to go back to our house. At least Marilyn was there.

On Wednesday, Carol was at the front door. Mom called me downstairs. "Patsy, please come here. Carol's here to see you." I didn't want to see her. But I didn't want a spanking, so I obeyed. My mom sat down and started reading a magazine.

Carol looked embarrassed. "Hi, Patsy."

"Hello." I glared at her.

"Please come over to my house."

I shook my head. "No."

"Patsy, my mother wants to see you," she pleaded.

I panicked. "No! Does your mom want to spank me too?"

Carol didn't stop. "Please, Patsy."

Mom looked up from her magazine, took a drag on her cigarette, and motioned with her head. "Go on, Patsy."

Feeling scared, mad, and even a little sick, I walked next door. I followed Carol past the porch swing with the tattered cushion and into her house.

Carol's mother smiled at me. "Patsy, here are some cookies. Let me get you and Carol some milk." I was confused and holding my body stiff, fearing that she would yell or, worse, spank me. After pouring two glasses of cold milk, she sat down with us at the kitchen table. It was hard for me to breathe.

"Patsy, I need to apologize. I'm sorry I didn't believe you." I felt my face get hot.

"I'm sorry, too, Patsy." Carol drew my gaze.

"Linda and her mom came by Sunday night. Linda said she was the one who pulled out the porch swing stuffing." I felt a tear roll down my face.

"You tried to tell us. I'm so sorry."

My head was swimming. Was I dreaming?

"Please eat your cookie, Patsy," Carol's mom urged me.

"Okay." The cookie stuck in my throat, and I couldn't really swallow it.

"I learned a lesson, Patsy. I need to know the facts before I accuse somebody."

"Okay." I forced a smile, but I didn't feel happy. A grown-up had never said they were sorry to me before. I knew I was right. I hated being called a liar, especially when doing the right thing. It should have felt better than it did.

> *I hated being called a liar, especially when doing the right thing.*

I walked back home with some cookies wrapped in waxed paper for my parents. Justice was served, but at what cost? I remember feeling so bleak. My mother never asked me what had happened at Carol's house, and to my knowledge, Carol's mom never mentioned to my mother that I'd been falsely accused. I suspect she didn't want to confront my mother and upset her in any way.

Aunt Evelyn brought my cousin Janny to Uncle Earl's house for a few days, and I was delighted. Marilyn, Janny, and I played in the yard, and the grown-ups sat in chairs on the porch talking. Skipping by my uncle, I chortled, "Hi, Crisscross Earl."

Before I knew it, my mother was on me, her voice raised. "Don't call people names, Patsy!" She grabbed my arm and yanked me up. I was puzzled. I didn't know what I had done.

Grandma Davis and Aunt Evelyn seemed equally uncertain about my mother's extreme behavior. I heard Aunt Evelyn say, "Don't spank her, Betty," as the stinging blow hit my bottom. She didn't listen to them. She spanked me right there in front of everyone.

I had to sit on the porch with the grown-ups, watching my cousins play—Janny and Marilyn used my jump rope and played tag. Aunt Evelyn let me use her handkerchief to wipe my tears. "Here you go, Patsy."

"Thanks. I wish I could play."

"Why did you call Earl cross, Patsy?"

My tears started again. "Aunt Evelyn, he's not cross Earl; he's Crisscross Earl. Look, his suspenders! They crisscross on his back."

She laughed a little, finally understanding what my eight-year-old "self" saw and meant. She stroked my head and comforted me but didn't explain the mistake to my mother for fear of setting her off again. Once again, my mother assumed I was guilty. She wouldn't listen to me or believe me when she did. Refusing to make eye contact with me for the rest of the day, my mother excluded me. I felt alone in my pain, without anyone who would stand up for me or protect me from my mother's irrational outbursts.

Looking back on this and other experiences of being falsely blamed by my mother with no one in my family protecting me from her wrath, I can see something positive resulted from it. A seed of justice was planted inside of me during these experiences of abuse and betrayal.

Is My Mother Dying?

I don't remember when I first noticed it, but from time to time, my house smelled funny. The odor would come and go. While my mother normally spent most of her time depressed in bed, there were times when she took to bed because she was ill. Each time she got sick, the odd smell would return. It was repulsive, and I kept my window open to keep that stinky air from overtaking my bedroom. Even in the winter, when it was freezing cold outside, I'd crack open my window when the smell was present. It wasn't until I was eight that I realized its origin.

After school one day, I walked in the back door, and the foul odor assaulted my senses. It was so intense I could almost taste it. As I opened the door, Grandma Davis was walking down the stairs with the laundry basket in her hands, and my appearance startled her.

"Oh, Patsy!" she cried, "Are you out of school so soon?"

"Why are you here?" I asked.

She stopped on the stairs, pulling the basket behind her as if trying to hide it. "Is that any way to greet your grandmother?" She looked offended.

I softened my voice. "Why are you doing laundry, Grandma? We do that on Saturday."

"I'm just here to help your mother. She isn't feeling well."

I closed the door behind me, my books under my arm. "That's nothing new. Mom usually isn't feeling well."

Grandma frowned. "Is that the way you should talk about your own mother? You should be ashamed of yourself. Your mother is genuinely sick. I took her to the doctor today."

I felt guilty. "Is she okay?"

My grandma glared at me. "She just had a very, very difficult day. That's all."

"I'm sorry, Grandma. Let me help with the washing." I reached up to take the basket from her.

She tucked the basket further behind her and shook her head. "Don't worry yourself about it. Go start your homework."

Obediently, I nodded and waited for her to descend the stairs so I could go to my room. As she passed me, I got a whiff of the stench. Whatever the smell was, it was now coming from the laundry basket that my grandmother was trying to hide from me.

I paused, watching her move past me toward the basement door. Balancing the basket on her hip, she reached out to open the door, and the basket tipped, dropping the contents on the floor.

I ran toward her to help pick up the soiled sheets and towels that had fallen, but Grandma tried to stop me. "No, Patsy. That's okay, I can take care of this." However, before she could scoop up the laundry, I saw the sheets were saturated with a dark red stain.

"Is that blood?" I cried out.

"Yes. Well, no. It's nothing," she stammered and quickly folded the sheets and towels to hide the redness.

"Is Mom bleeding? Shouldn't we get her to the hospital?"

"Patsy, stop asking so many questions!"

"But what's going on?" I was gripped with fear. "Is Mom going to die?"

Grandma pulled my hand away from the laundry. "No, Patsy. She is not going to die. But she is sick. So please let me take care of this, and go do your homework."

I stared at her.

"Your mother just needs to rest." She didn't move until I started up the stairs. I made my way to the top and peered around the door into my mother's room. I stared at her sleeping face. She was pretty, sort of like Snow White, with pale skin and dark hair. I longed to crawl into bed with her and have her hold me like Aunt Gertrude used to do when I was little. I moved closer to her, but I was sickened by the odor again. *It's the smell of blood! Why would my mother bleed like this?*

I was left trying to connect the dots of my family's puzzle.

I had yet to learn about menstrual cycles or conditions some women may have. My only frame of reference was watching my Grandma Stroberg being eaten away by cancer. Fear rippled through me as I wondered about it all. *Is Grandma Davis telling me the truth? Is Mom okay, or is she dying like Gramma Stroberg?* Once again, I was left trying to connect the dots of my family's puzzle. The hush of grown-ups, avoidant behaviors, and lack of healthy explanations left me anxious and feeling more alone.

I Don't Want a Little Brother

I had settled on my bed to do my homework when my father stuck his head into my bedroom door. "Patsy, I want you to stay with Aunt Gertrude for a while."

"How long?" I asked, hoping it would be for the rest of my life. Even though I had turned nine, I still longed to live on the other side of the duplex, like I had when I was a toddler.

"Just a few hours," he said. "Or maybe until tomorrow. I'm not sure. But gather up what you need in case you have to spend the night. And hurry." He disappeared before I could ask what was going on.

I quickly pulled out my blue canvas bag and packed some pajamas and barely got my books together when he returned. "Let's go."

Following behind him, we rushed downstairs, out the back door, and across the back porch to the other side of the duplex. A quick rap on the door brought Aunt Gertrude, who invited us in. "It's time," he said.

She nodded. "Patsy can stay as long as needed."

Dad disappeared without explanation. I was about to ask what it was time for when Aunt Gertrude said, "Are you hungry, Patsy?

Want a snack?" I nodded yes, and off we went to the kitchen as if everything that needed to be said had been said. I spent the remainder of the day and night playing with Marilyn, and Aunt Gertrude got me off for school the next day.

When I got home from school, my back door was locked, with no sign of my parents. I knocked on Aunt Gertrude's door, and she smiled, welcoming me in. "Your parents aren't back from the hospital yet."

"The hospital?" I was alarmed. "Is Mommy okay? Is she sick?" All that blood I saw may mean she was dangerously sick.

She smiled sweetly at me. "Oh, dear, I didn't mean to scare you! Your mom is at the hospital having a baby!"

I knew that moms had babies, but I didn't know *my mom* was having one. Unclear about how all that came about, I stood there, mouth open in total surprise.

"Aren't you excited about getting a new brother or sister?"

How could I get excited about something no one had told me about? I just nodded. "Can I go play with Marilyn?"

"Certainly, honey. I'll let you know when your parents get back."

Looking back on this experience, I find it hard to accept that I had no idea I was about to become a big sister. Wouldn't someone have said something to me? Hadn't there been some plans made that would have prepared me for this huge change in our family? A crib bought or a baby shower held? Wouldn't I have noticed my mother's stomach was growing or that she might complain of back pains or fatigue? And yet, this is how I remember this day. I was taken completely off guard.

No one, not even my Aunt Gertrude, took the time to explain to me what was happening in their adult lives. I was repeatedly ignored by those I relied on—but why? Because they didn't care about me? Perhaps, but I believe my father and my aunt truly loved me. I think my family was a product of the time. Children were considered too young to understand. Maybe they simply thought they were private people who didn't talk about personal things. Regardless of the reason, one awful surprise after another befell me, and I developed an intense desire to know and tell the truth.

Right before dinner, I heard a commotion downstairs, and Marilyn and I came down to investigate. My dad was standing in the doorway with a handful of cigars, beaming with the goofiest smile on his face. "It's a boy! Allen Paul Stroberg!"

Uncle Alvar slapped him on the back and took one of the cigars. Aunt Gertrude clapped her hands like a delighted little girl. "I'll have to add August twenty-first, nineteen-forty-eight, to our birthday list!"

She saw us standing there. "Patsy! You have a baby brother!"

I looked around the room for the baby. "Oh, no, dear, your mother and brother will stay in the hospital for a week or so. You can stay here with us because your dad has to work."

I didn't particularly want a little brother, but I preferred staying here rather than at home.

My father hugged me and kissed the top of my head. "Don't worry, honey. You won't have to stay here long. I think they can come home in three or four days."

Worry about time away from my mother? That wasn't what I was feeling at all.

When I got home Tuesday afternoon from school, I could hear a baby crying from our side of the duplex. I rolled my eyes. *A new baby brother that cries.* From bad to worse.

Entering the back door, I saw a sight I'll never forget. My mother sat on the couch with a tiny baby wrapped up tight in a light blue blanket. The expression on her face was one I'd never seen before. She was smiling. No, not just smiling, but glowing. She had a look of love on her face. She had never, ever looked at me that way.

I stumbled back, my stomach souring.

The room quickly filled up with Aunt Gertrude and Uncle Alvar; Grandma and Grandpa Davis soon arrived, with Aunt Evelyn in tow.

"Don't just stand in the door. Come see your baby brother, Patsy," my dad said, coming into the room with a tray of drinks. I didn't want to.

"Patsy!" my mother scolded me, her stern expression returning. "Come over here and kiss Allie." Quickly, I walked over and met my brother. He was tiny, with a face framed by short reddish-blond hair. I awkwardly kissed the little creature on the forehead.

She had a look of love on her face. She had never, ever looked at me that way.

Having fulfilled my duty, no one paid any further attention to me. I grabbed my books and climbed the stairs up to my room.

Falling onto my bed, I grabbed my pillow and pulled it closely around my head, trying to block out the voices of happiness rising from downstairs.

I Wish I Could Fly Away

The happy sounds of my mother playing with Allie in the living room were more than I could bear. Using my toe, I pushed my bedroom door closed without having to get off my bed. I closed my eyes as tears squeezed out the corners. I knew that both of my parents loved Allie. And I knew that my father loved me. But my mother's rejection, the loneliness, the pain of every breath of life was excruciating. *How do I stop this pain? How can I stop it forever?*

I knew there was only one answer. *My suffering won't end until I die. But I might live for a long, long time.*

That realization pressed down on me like a suffocating weight. *No! I can't wait that long!*

My mind immediately set to solving the problem. *I could shoot myself, but I don't have a gun. Someone would find out and stop me if I tried to get one.*

I rolled over and buried my head in the pillow. *There's poison. We have rat poison in the basement. And there's also bleach down there. No, I'd suffer dying that way.* Once, I stumbled onto a rat that had been poisoned—before my dad could put him in the trash. Awful. All twisted and bent in agony. *No, I'm trying to end my pain, not suffer more. It's got to be quick and painless.*

After weeks of exploration, I figured out the solution. I stood tall at my bedroom window. I always loved looking out through the trees. Our house had high ceilings, which made my second-floor bedroom rise high above the yards and sidewalks in our neighborhood. I often imagined being one of the birds who could fly. I wished I could fly away.

I waited until both Allie and Mom were sleeping after lunch, then returned to my bedroom. Sliding the big window open, the lilac breeze met me. I looked down at the cement sidewalk under my window and stared at the gray hardness directly beneath me. It was a long, long way down. I knew exactly how I could get free of my mother and my pain simultaneously.

I wished I could fly away.

I put one leg over the windowsill and paused. I wasn't scared. I was determined. *It will be easy. Just lean over, Patsy. Put your head down and let go.* Was there anything I'd forgotten to consider? *You'll fall, and your head will hit first, cracking open. Dead on contact. You'll be free.*

I pulled the other leg carefully outside and sat on the sill. *Just lean over, Patsy, and let go.*

Sitting on the window ledge, with both legs dangling, I let go with one hand. *Imagine no more loneliness. Just lean forward and let go with the other hand. You'll be dead before you know it.* My fingers tingled in anticipation.

I paused. *Wait! Is there anything I have forgotten? What if I don't die? What if I only break my legs?* My breath caught in my throat. The voice inside my head continued. *You might not be able to talk or walk, and then what?* I knew the answer to that question. *I'd never be able to get away from her!*

The image of being in a bed, utterly dependent on my mother, stopped me short. A scene appeared in my mind. I am in soiled diapers, hungry and scared. I cry out for her, but I sound like a wild, wounded beast. No words, just noise. She never responds to my groaning. I'm alone and trapped, and my suffering is even worse because of my utter dependency on her.

I pulled away from the window, afraid now that I might accidentally fall. *No! I have to stay alive. Someday, I'll be old enough to leave her behind.* And then a strange thought came to mind. *There is a time for us all to die. You will die when you are forty-three.* Where did that come from? Eventually, with a deep breath of surrender and my legs back in the room, the window descended and so did any hope of immediate relief. But I did have hope that someday my suffering would end. Falling onto my bed, I cried, grieving the life I could not escape. Between sobs, the sounds of the sweet laughter and tenderness my brother and mom shared echoed in my ears.

The Fur and the Fire

Grandma Davis and Grandpa Roy lived in a small, rounded trailer built to be moved. Only my grandparents' trailer never did. It sat along rows of others in a crowded trailer park that backed up to the highway. I think my Grandpa Roy might have picked this location for the singular reason that a beer joint sat four trailers away from theirs, and he could easily walk there and back.

The dingy trailer smelled of cigarettes and stale beer, but I loved being there. One benefit was escaping my mother's constant whiny demands. "Patsy, get me a glass of water," or "Patsy, bring me another blanket." In addition, I got to be with my adoring Grandma Davis, who lavished me with affection and attention.

While my grandmother was a source of great nurturance, my grandfather was kind but distant and, as I learned later, wasted whatever money they had on booze and get-rich-quick schemes. He told me, "Patsy, my ship is about to come in," which confused me since we weren't anywhere near the water. If I had any feelings connected to him, it was protectiveness of my Grandma Davis when he said something unkind. She would be so sad; sometimes, she would cry.

On one particular occasion, my Aunt Jett, Grandma's sister, was going to perm my hair in her shop late in the afternoon, followed by an overnight in the trailer.

I had to sit still for a long time while Aunt Jett slid my hair through a form and rolled it on a metal cylinder. Somehow, the tubes connected above my head to a machine. It smelled horrible—burning hair and chemicals. My scalp felt like it was on fire. When the process ended, my straight hair was now fuzzy and curly. I was happy to be done and get back to the trailer.

It was getting dark by the time my grandmother wiggled a small key and opened the trailer door wide for me. I felt like the trailer was smiling at me, welcoming me inside. With my scalp still burning, I dashed up the three steps and headed for the small bed stuffed in the rear. Holding my arms wide, I flung myself back onto the bed with a freedom I rarely felt as a child.

Grandma Davis smiled and gave me a little wink. "Don't get too comfortable." I pulled myself up on my knees, clapped my hands, and squealed. I watched as my grandmother slid open the closet door and took out her prized possession—her authentic rabbit fur coat. Over the years, it was the one item that she had never allowed Grandpa Roy to hock or drink away. She carefully removed it from the cloth covering that protected the old and worn coat and spread it out tenderly on the top of the bed. It was pure luxury. "Here you go, Patsy,"

Holding my arms wide, I flung myself back onto the bed with a freedom I rarely felt as a child.

I gently ran my hands through the luscious fur, letting it slide between my fingers. It was so soft. My grandmother took a few steps, thereby arriving in the kitchen area. She pulled a pack of cigarettes from her purse, lit one, and started fixing dinner—the pan in one hand and the cigarette in the other. I enjoyed myself in the folds of the coat.

The door slammed open, and Grandpa stomped in, causing us both to jump slightly. He took off his hat and saw me on his bed, but there was no flicker of acknowledgment in his eyes. "Woman, I'm going to wet my whistle, so don't cook anything for me."

She frowned and took a drag on her cigarette but said nothing.

He asked, "Are you coming along to make sure I don't get into *trouble?*"

As she kept her silence, he looked over at me and smiled. "I don't imagine you could go to the bar with me tonight, right Patsy?"

I couldn't tell if he was joking or asking me an honest question. My gaze went back and forth between them, searching for how to respond.

He patted me gently on the head. "I'm just joshing you, Patsy. Where I'm going isn't a place for a nice girl like you."

Grandma Davis crossed her arms. "I suppose not."

Grandpa Roy jammed his hat back onto his head and snarled as the door closed behind him, "Don't wait up."

After dinner, I brushed my teeth while looking in the bathroom mirror at my curly hair. I changed into my pajamas and pivoted into the kitchen. I got a glass, filled it with water, and then looked around for crackers. "Grandma? Do you have any crackers?"

She poked her head into the kitchen. "I usually do. Let me look." She moved things around in the cupboard and found an opened box of soda crackers. "Why do you want these? Are you hungry?"

I shook my head. "No, but I always make sure I have crackers and water by my bed each night. And I have an extra blanket on my bed."

Grandma gave me a strange look as she handed me some crackers. "Whatever for, Patsy? Don't you get enough dinner?"

I took them and the glass of water, put them on the bedstand, and crawled back onto the bed. Shrugging, I said, "I don't know why, Grandma, but I always do."

I sunk back into the softness of the fur coat and sighed with contentment. "Will you read me more of *Black Beauty*?"

Grandma gave me an odd look. "I certainly will." She pulled open a drawer where she kept a couple of books for me and handed *Black Beauty* to me. "Figure out where we left off and then move over."

I handed her back the book with the regal horse on the cover, my finger marking where to start reading. I scooted over so she could get in bed beside me. I snuggled up next to her, warm and cozy. She lit another cigarette and began to read. Her soft voice filled the room, and I drifted off to sleep before she finished the first page.

Sometime later, I woke up slowly, as if in a haze. It took a few blinks before I realized the fog was smoke! The end of the bed beneath me was burning. I shook Grandma Davis awake. "Fire!" I screamed.

She jolted up just as the flames erupted like spears leaping into the air between us. I pulled away into the corner of the bed, afraid to move. Fortunately, there wasn't much distance between the burning bed and the kitchen sink. Grandma threw one pan-full of water onto the corner of the bed, and the fire smoldered out a bit. The sizzling noise and the smell terrified me as I hunkered against the wall on the other end of the mattress.

"Come here now, Patsy!" she yelled.

"No, I'm afraid!"

She didn't hesitate. She reached across the soggy and smoldering bed, grabbed my arm, and dragged me screaming across the mattress with one hand. With her other hand, she rescued her fur coat. Dumping us both on the floor, she yelled, "Run outside!" Shoving her fur into my arms, she added, "And, take this with you!"

I spun on my heels and ran barefoot out of the trailer. "Grandma! Grandma!" Turning around, I screamed, "Fire! Help! Help!"

From outside, smoke was pouring out the front door, and there was a smell of burning foam. Neighbors, who were awakened by my cries, ran over to help. "Call the fire department!" someone yelled. "Do you have a hose? Where's the water pump?"

Emerging from the smoky trailer, my grandmother's sweaty face appeared. "It's okay. I got it out. Would one of you be willing to go over to the bar and get my husband?"

One of the men hollered, "I'll get Roy for ya." And the crowd dispersed.

My grandmother walked down the three steps and put her arms around me. We both cried. "Oh, my precious child. I don't want to imagine what could have happened to us tonight."

The firetruck arrived about the same time that Grandpa Roy stumbled up to us. "What did you do? Smoke in bed again?"

She glared at him, and for once, he backed down.

He grabbed me and said through his alcohol-laced breath, "You okay, Patsy?"

I nodded but started to cry again. Grandma pulled me into her arms and held me tight.

"Step away from the trailer!" the fireman ordered.

"It's out now. Thank you for coming." Grandma watched as the fireman inspected the home and concurred there was nothing left burning. All that was left was a smoldering wet mattress and a smoky mess.

By the time the firetruck left, Grandpa Roy seemed to have sobered up. "I'll go over to the bar and call Al. He'll want to come get her after all of this."

Sharing her rabbit coat over our nightgowns and robes, we walked around the circle of mobile homes, waiting for my father to appear. Despite the danger of the fire, I felt safe with her. I clung to my grandmother's hand as if my life depended on it—because it had.

Why Are We Living in a Hospital?

It was the only place I'd ever remembered living, the duplex on the corner of Westdrop and 142nd, Cleveland, Ohio. And now, we all had to move. Aunt Gertrude, Uncle Alvar, and Marilyn left for the new home they had built in Mayfield. I knew I would miss them, but Dad had been working on building us a new house on Beachview near Metropolitan Park. Not ready yet, it was still so exciting to think of moving to a brand-new home!

In the between time, we moved around a lot. First, after we left the duplex, we stayed with Aunt Evelyn in Twinsburg. After having tonsilitis so often, I had surgery to remove them, plus my adenoids. Aunt Evelyn took care of me. And I had to change schools. Since I was shy, it was hard to make new friends. I ate lunch alone and read my book. Then we went to Uncle Earl's for summer vacation months. But my dad was still working on the new house, so we ended up at an apartment in a condemned hospital because my mother didn't want to spend any money on renting a nicer place. It was cheap. She always saved money for her parents, taking from our household to provide for them.

We moved to a room in a large hospital that was no longer functioning as a hospital. Part of it was condemned, and the remainder was now rooms for rent. The massive building wasn't exactly warm and inviting, being gray on the outside and the inside. The walls, the floors, the stairs, and every door were gray. Everything looked the same, so I often got lost and frightened, trying to find our gray door. My imagination went wild during those moments.

I had to change schools. Since I was shy, it was hard to make new friends. I ate lunch alone and read my book.

We had one big room, now our home, number 2411. Transient families packed the building, living together in single rooms and sharing a lone kitchen on the far end of our hall. With so many people, especially babies and elderly, in such a small space, there were always lots of smells and noises.

When I complained, my mother told me I should be grateful to have a roof over my head. "Patsy, I lived through the Depression. I only had bread with sugar on it once a day, and we were homeless. We huddled together under a tent. You should be grateful to have this room to live in."

No matter what Mom said, I didn't feel grateful. I was eleven, and changing schools in the middle of the year was very stressful for me. I would sit at lunch in hopes that someone would talk to me. I pulled inward even more.

One bright spot in the big hospital was the attention I received when I would hang out in the communal kitchen, and some of the ladies tried to teach me things. They'd say, "This is the right way to clean the counter, Patsy." "You're not doing it right. You need to scrape the dried egg off the tines of the fork, Patsy." "Remember, whenever you eat eggs, put the silverware in water to soak right away.

Then it cleans up real easy." I didn't mind them telling me what to do. I felt that they were helping me to grow up and do things right.

Mom would come down to fill her thermos with coffee and warm up Chef Boyardee for Allie and me, but she never seemed to notice what was going on with me.

I made one friend while we lived there. Her name was Sheila. We were both eleven and ran up and down the staircases and through the long hallways. I'd skip stairs from one landing to the next of the great cement stairway. "Sheila! Look how many steps I can jump down at one time."

"Yeah, but can you slide down the railing?" She always needed to be better than me.

And she teased me a lot. "My apartment is bigger than yours, Patsy!"

"I don't care."

"I have a new mint green sweater."

"I don't care."

"My cousin has a pogo-stick."

"I don't care, Sheila!"

My dad called her an arrogant little girl, but I wasn't supposed to tell her.

Sheila and I would sit on the big cement steps together since neither of us had rooms big enough for company. "Let's write down all the songs we can remember."

"Let's see if we can come up with a hundred!" It helped make the day go by until dinnertime.

I looked forward to our family's Sunday drives to escape the dreary world where we lived. But most Sunday afternoons were ruined by my parents' incessant arguing. No matter what the topic was, they would bicker the whole time.

"Al, turn left."

"I know where we are going, Betty. Stop giving me directions."

"You should have turned back there, Al."

Finally, I'd interrupt. "Can we go home? I think I'm carsick."

Dad would start to speak up, but then he'd clench his jaw, and his cheeks held all his rage. I always had a stomachache by the end of the drive. I wasn't car sick but parent sick.

During the week, we didn't see my dad much. He worked all day at the gas station and then went to Beachview to get more done on our new house he was building. Occasionally, my mother would take us over there in the evenings. But it didn't take long before another argument heated up. Mom would tell Allie and me to wait in the car while she and Dad had words. Mom seemed so indifferent about our new home, but I couldn't wait to get to Beachview and live somewhere other than our hospital apartment, which I hated.

Pork Chops on the Stove

Even though I had to change schools again and do so in the middle of the year, I was delighted when we moved on a cold November day. Finally, we were together in the new house on Beachview. Our neighbor used Dad's camera as we posed for a photograph together on that chilly afternoon. Propped in between Mom and Dad, my brother and I were tall, skinny kids of two and eleven. Wearing the scarves Aunt Gertrude knit, Mom fussed with Allie's straight blond hair, combing it to the side. My strawberry blond curls framed my face under my hat. Excited about our new house standing behind us, the four of us smiled for the camera.

Our house faced Metropolitan Park, across the street down a steep hill. Allie and I each had a room. My room was upstairs and had a large window overlooking the fall-colored trees in our backyard and those of our neighbor's. My bed, a wooden chair, a closet, and a bedside table with a lamp filled the room. It was a spectacular house in every way—perhaps most importantly because my father had built it with his own hands.

I expected to see more of my father in the evenings once we moved in, but that didn't happen. I asked my mom, "Is Dad working late?"

"No, not at his station," she replied. "He's building a house for your grandparents. They don't want to live in that trailer anymore."

My dad amazed me. His kindness, hard work, and devotion to family were exemplary. It took a few more months, but Grandpa Roy and Grandma Davis could soon move into their new home on Melville Street. All of us were finally able to settle in.

My room was the last one Dad finished. Unfinished walls surrounded me for over a year, but I didn't mind. I used a cross beam as a bookshelf, and there was a perfect cubby hole, out of sight, for my diary. After my dad completed the Melville house for our grandparents, Allie and I finally stopped using blankets as window coverings. Aunt Evelyn fixed her old green drapes to fit our windows. I hoped things would get better between my parents in this new home. Maybe the bickering would stop? If only my mother felt some gratitude for what Dad had done for us and her parents.

I was taking a class at the Lutheran Church once a week to prepare for Confirmation. I had to take the Cleveland city bus to the church across town. A skinny and timid kid, I was afraid of people *all* the time. (Today, they would call me socially awkward.) It was a big deal for me to take the bus. That first week, I mustered my strength and courage and managed to get on, dropped my nickel in the slot, and sat quietly as close to the driver as possible.

I looked at the others on the bus. I observed and analyzed each person—this might have been where I learned to size people up. There was the businessman with his briefcase and shiny shoes. An old lady wore a pilled winter coat even though it was so hot. I saw a sighing mother with her two children, fussing at their coats and wiping their noses. There was an older man with a cane. One glamorous lady smelled nice, and her skirt whooshed as she walked by. And a kind elderly lady carried a book and smiled at everyone. As I watched, I felt self-conscious. I worried that someone would need to sit next to me or, even worse, talk to me.

I am still unsure how it happened—maybe I was thinking about a lesson from Confirmation class—but I had a revelation during an afternoon bus ride one day. It occurred to me that while I was quiet and shy, those passengers had problems too. I was not the only one. I courageously looked up at the faces of those riding with me. *A lot of them are probably more afraid than I am about something. And they are alone.*

I don't know why, but that moment changed me. I started to truly *see* others—more than I worried about how they saw me. I changed. I started smiling more. To my surprise, people smiled back. It was almost easy to be friendly. Saying hello to others became my norm. I stopped looking at shoes and focused on faces. It was an epiphany and where I became powerful inside.

I wasn't so scared anymore.

Every night, I hung the dress I chose for the next day on the doorknob of the closet and put my undershirt, socks, and sweater on the wooden chair before crawling into bed. In the morning, I raced to get dressed quickly. When I awoke, I would reach for my school clothes and pull them into bed with me. The warmth there took the chill off the fabric, and I slipped into the day's outfit. Aunt Gertrude taught me this trick years earlier for those bone-chilling mornings.

I was always awake before my mom, and after I got dressed, I'd go into the kitchen and pour my Cheerios. Sometimes, she would shuffle to the kitchen, pour a cup of coffee from Dad's pot, and stare at me while I finished my cereal. Other times, she'd be in bed sleeping. I would go into her room and say goodbye because I knew I had to leave the house at eight to get to school on time. She would lean up on one elbow and look at me. "Bye, honey. Now comb your hair before you leave, Patsy."

I walked home from school one afternoon, lost in a daydream about taking horseback riding lessons the following summer. I imagined myself on the back of a glorious horse like my friend's Captain, a Tennessee Walker, riding with the ease of a great horsewoman. But as soon as I opened the creaky back door and walked into my house, I knew something was very wrong. The house smelled of cooking meat, which it never did at that time of day. It was way too early to start making dinner. I dropped my books on the floor and ran directly into my parents' room. "Mom?" Her side of the closet door was wide open; she and all her clothes were gone.

I dashed to Allie's room, wondering if she had left him behind. But his closet was stripped bare. The drawers of his dresser were pulled out and empty. His toys were gone. His books and his special train blanket were gone. I ran into the bathroom. Her side of the medicine cabinet, makeup, she had taken everything. No note. No advanced warning. They were gone. I whispered my worry. "Allie! Allie? Allie. Allie, please be safe."

Trying to catch my breath, I stumbled back into the kitchen to pick up my books and saw a covered pan on the stove. Without looking, I already knew what was in there—pork chops with potatoes. My dad's favorite. Mom had abandoned us, taken away my three-year-old brother, yet had the presence of mind to cook Dad his favorite meal? Of course, I was supposed to heat it for him. At least I had some role in her selfish little scenario. But why did she leave us dinner? Was this her way of trying to make it easier? Or to torture him? But then, why did she do anything if not for herself?

"Mommy! Mommy, don't leave me," I cried out. But it was useless for me to plead. She was already gone.

The afternoon was almost unbearable. I sat frozen. Alone. I stared out the window, trying to figure out what this meant. The numbness I knew so well was disturbed. I was angry. I was angry with myself for being so upset. I hated her. And yet, I desperately wanted her to love me. *How could you leave me like this? What did I ever do to make you hate me so much? Allie better be okay. Where are you, Mom?*

My father walked in the door at five-thirty, as always. I had already heated the pork chops and potatoes and had them on his plate. I stood there, not knowing what to say, with red-rimmed eyes that had cried themselves dry. He looked at me and paled slightly. "What happened?"

"They're gone. Mom took Allie and left."

He did exactly what I had done. First, he rushed to their bedroom. His footsteps were slower when he walked to Allie's room. It seemed a long time before I heard him shuffle back into the kitchen.

"She left us dinner," I said as if that was some consolation prize. "I heated it up for you." I nodded toward the plate.

He dropped into his chair. Placing an elbow on either side of his plate, he held his head in his hands. I sat down quietly in my chair. I wasn't hungry, so there was no plate for me. We sat in silence as he ate. It seemed like he shrank in size and stature as if my mother had sucked the strength out of his body. If it weren't for the modified brace he still wore, I feared he might have withered into a little old man in front of my eyes.

After about ten minutes, he pushed his almost full plate away. Pulling a pack of cigarettes from his shirt pocket, he lit one but didn't put it into his mouth. He just let it smolder in the ashtray.

Finally, Dad stood and walked across the room. He looked back at me and said, "That's just who she is, Patsy." He went down the hall toward his half-empty room.

He'd left the cigarette in the ashtray where he'd been sitting. I squished the life out of it. I started to place the untouched pork chops in a casserole dish to store in the fridge but then decided I hated pork chops, and I dumped them into the trash. Washing his plate and the skillet, locking up the house, and turning off the lights, I went upstairs, into my room, and closed the door—not only to my bedroom but to my heart.

16

I Don't Want You Either

I spooned some bacon grease over the eggs—sunny side up, the way Dad liked them. A pop of grease from the bacon landed on my hand. "Oh, that hurts!" I said to no one, shaking my hand. The coffee percolated as the clock read five-fifteen a.m.—very early for a twelve-year-old to get up, fix her dad a hot meal, and pack his lunch before he went to work. In my mother's absence, that job fell to me.

I wouldn't say I liked getting up when it was still dark, but it was a trade-off that came with benefits. No more scary arguments between my parents. No more waiting on my mother in her smelly bedroom. And no more "Patsy, will you feed the baby?" or "Patsy, will you change Allie's diapers?"

Dad would come out to eat, and I'd stagger back into my bedroom to catch a little more sleep before getting myself up and out to school. In the haze of early morning cooking, I realized I didn't miss my mother. I also didn't miss caring for Allie. However, I did feel horrible about her taking Allie with her and leaving me behind. I hadn't seen her since she left as she made no effort to get in touch with me.

Try as I may, I couldn't push the questions out of my mind. *Why would you leave me behind and never say goodbye? What did I do to make you hate me so much? Will I ever see you again?*

The phone's shrill ring pierced the silent darkness, abruptly pulling me out of a deep sleep. Who would call in the middle of the night? I pulled back my covers and grabbed my robe. I hurried to get it around me before being engulfed by the coldness of the winter night.

"Hello?" I heard my dad's sleepy voice downstairs in the living room.

I walked down to join him. *Is someone sick? Has someone died?* My father's face suddenly grew darker. "Again?" He listened to the response. "Where do you live?" He paused. "I know right where that is. I'll be there in ten minutes."

He hung up the phone, then jumped slightly at seeing me. "Oh, I didn't know you were there."

"What's wrong, Dad?"

"A woman who lives near your Grandma Davis found Allie wandering down the street on Melville in front of her house."

I looked outside at the bitter night. "This is the third time, Dad. And in this weather! It's snowing."

He nodded sadly. "In only his pj's and a very wet diaper."

"Is he okay?"

"Yes." He turned abruptly. "I've got to get dressed and go get him."

"Why was he outside by himself? Where is…" I stopped before I uttered, "…Mom."

He shook his head in dismayed disbelief. "I don't know why it surprises me, but it still does."

"Want me to come with you?" I asked.

"No, Patsy." He laid his hand on my shoulder. "Go back to bed. You need your rest for school tomorrow. He can sleep with me tonight while we sort this out."

A few weeks later, my father told me as he left for work, "There will be a woman coming here today to talk to you."

"What kind of woman?" I asked.

"A social worker. She works with the court here."

"Court?" I stepped back anxiously. "I haven't done anything wrong. Is she going to arrest me?"

He smiled sadly. "Oh no, Patsy, you have done nothing wrong." He fidgeted with the coins in his pocket for a moment. "It's because your mother and I are getting a divorce." He watched me soak in the information. "The judge will decide where you and Allie will live."

Alarmed, I cried, "What? I want to stay with you!"

He put his hand on my shoulder. "I know you do, and I want you to live with me. Just tell the social worker what you want." My mind was swirling with rage at my mother. Dad kept talking. "The state of Ohio and the judge will probably go with the lady's recommendation."

Turning to leave, he reminded me, "She'll be here at four after you get home from school. Wear something nice." And he left.

Frowning, I repeated what my father had said with disdain. "The judge will *probably* go with her recommendation." *Probably? I am not going to live with my mother! I won't.* Having made that decision, I got ready for school and left for the day.

I would have been more horribly distressed had I known that fathers rarely got full custody of their children at that time. The courts were strongly biased in favor of mothers. I was older, and the judge might listen to my opinion, but it was unlikely that my father would get custody of my little brother. He was only four.

After school, I changed into a pretty dress, combed my hair, and tried to look well cared for. "I'll show this lady what a great dad he is." A few minutes before four, I walked down the stairs. Seeing the front door ajar, I tip-toed quietly to it and saw my dad and Aunt Evelyn sitting side by side on the porch steps.

"Al, don't worry. I will testify on your behalf," Evelyn assured my father. When he didn't respond, she pressed in further. "Betty might be my sister, but I know what she's been up to. Those children do not belong with her." I knew I shouldn't eavesdrop, but I listened with all my might. "She's going out every night dancing and drinking. And you know, as much as our mother loves Patsy, she's too busy trying to keep my daddy from spending time with that bar girl to watch after a young boy like Allie." My mind was racing with this information I wasn't supposed to know.

My father took a deep breath. "Thank you, Evelyn. You know that a father rarely gets full custody of their children. The odds are against me. But I want to keep our family together."

"Well, I am for you. I'll tell them about the other men and syphilis."

My dad's head dropped, and he stared at his shoes silently.

"Al..."

Looking up, he said, "Oh, I know about the men."

She sighed heavily. "Honestly, Al, I don't know why you haven't divorced her."

Before he could respond or notice that I'd heard them, a plump but cheery-looking woman appeared at the base of the stairs. "Albert Stroberg?" she asked.

Jumping to his feet, he said, "Yes. That's me. This is Evelyn Lundblad, my sister-in-law." Evelyn nodded as she got up from the step.

"Good to meet you both. I am Miss Chansler, with the State of Ohio. I'm here to talk with," she looked down at her notes, "a Miss Patricia Stroberg. Your daughter, isn't that right?" Miss Chansler asked. I moved backward, away from the door, then silently eased back into the living room so it appeared I was entering it.

"Yes, she's inside."

Aunt Evelyn stifled a cough. "Well, I will leave you to it," she said, heading for her car.

My dad was focused on Miss Chansler. "Come on in, please." My father led the way up the porch steps and opened the door to let Miss Chansler enter first. She looked up and saw me on the opposite side of the living room. Reaching out her hand, she walked in my direction. "Good to meet you, Patricia. I'm Miss Chansler."

We shook hands, and I stood there, anxiously awaiting orders.

My father motioned to the couch and chair. "Please, make yourself comfortable," and we sorted out that I would sit on the sofa and she on the chair. "You will please excuse us, won't you, Mr. Stroberg? This is a confidential meeting."

"Oh yes." My father's face reddened. "I will be in the kitchen if you need me."

Once my father was out of earshot, she asked if I knew why she was there. "I think my parents are getting a divorce."

She nodded. "And the judge in this case has many important decisions to make that will affect you. I am here to let the judge know what you need and want to happen in the future."

"I want to live with my dad!" I blurted out.

She looked a bit surprised but nodded her head. "Patricia, tell me more about why you want to continue to live here."

I leaned back as if preparing to give a speech. "My mother left me—left us. I came home from school, and she had taken my baby brother and her things and was gone."

"Did she leave a note or give you any explanation?"

Shaking my head vehemently, I said, "No! Nothing. And I haven't seen her since. She hasn't come by to see me or call me!" I crossed my arms. "She just left." I felt the hot poker in my heart. I hated this feeling. It made my breathing hard and my eyes water.

I bit my lower lip, tried to take a deep breath, and declared, "I want to live with my father because he takes care of me and loves me. Mom doesn't even like me. She left without me and never said goodbye."

"I know this has been a hard time for you."

"You have no idea! Before my mother left, I had to help my little brother all the time. I helped him get dressed in the morning, fed him, and gave him his bath at night. She did nothing! I got so frustrated. He could make me so mad! I didn't want to be his mom!" Surprised by my heightened tone and honesty, I wondered if I'd said too much.

I want to live with my father because he takes care of me and loves me.

I looked straight at Miss Chansler. "I don't think she ever wanted to be my mom. And…"

"Yes, Patricia?"

"I know she goes dancing and drinking a lot."

Her gaze was locked on me, and she kept nodding, keeping rhythm with my words. She looked down at her notes and then back up at me. "Okay, young lady. I understand. I'm not sure where you got your information, but you have been very clear about where you want to live."

"I want to live with my dad. You'll tell people who make the decisions, right?"

She smiled at me, "Yes, Patricia, I will."

I got very quiet.

She asked, "Is there anything else you want me to tell the judge?"

My eyes got moist, and my voice quivered. "Please tell the judge that if he decides to make me live with my mother…"

"Yes?"

"I don't think Mom would listen to the judge. She probably wouldn't let me stay with her even if the judge said she had to. Tell him that she doesn't want me. She doesn't love me." My throat burned as I tried not to cry. I drew a deep breath. "And I don't know what I did wrong to make her not want to love me." Finally, tears spilled down my cheeks.

A sadness fell over the social worker's face. She patted my hand. "You have done nothing wrong, Patricia. I'll do everything I can to ensure you stay right here with your father." Packing up her things, she said, "Clearly, this is where you belong."

Moms for Hire

It was a relief to know that Allie and I would live with my dad. But that meant that my brother's care fell primarily on my shoulders. I resented my brother because my mom took him when she disappeared and left me behind. Now my resentment grew as I was expected to step in as his principal caretaker.

The anger I felt toward him came to a head one evening. Allie was four, and it was bath time. Plastic cups were yet to be invented, so I brought in a glass to rinse his hair. "Don't touch it!" I warned him. I turned around for a towel and heard the crash of shattering glass.

He sat back against the tub with fear in his eyes. "Allie!" I yelled. I was furious that he had disobeyed me and could get cut. He raised his arms in front of his face to shield himself from getting hit. I stopped cold.

My heart ached for him. He was afraid of me. I leaned over the tub and hugged him. "I won't hurt you, Allie. Just sit in the tub while I clean up the glass." I swept up the shards, making sure it was safe to walk on the floor. I put the towel around him and realized something I couldn't see before. *Mom abandoned me, but he doesn't have a mom either.* If I kept resenting my brother, and it showed, he would grow up and hate me. So I decided to be nicer to him from then on. He does not remember this, which is just as well. But deciding to be kind to Allie was a big turning point for me. I realized that I could decide what kind of big sister I wanted to be.

"I want you to meet Miss Anderson," my father said. He opened the door to a young woman. She wore a red checkered blouse like my friend Linda's mom wore.

She smiled nervously. "You must be Patsy," she said, reaching out her hand to me.

I shook her hand but said nothing, giving her a suspicious look.

Ignoring my unwelcoming demeanor, she stooped down to Allie playing on the living room floor. "Good to meet you, Allie."

He grinned at her, happy to see anyone who would pay attention to him. After that most recent late-night call for Dad to rescue him, Allie moved back in with us.

My dad looked at her and smiled and then smiled at me. "Miss Anderson will be here when you get home from school, and she will take care of Allie."

Suddenly, I liked this woman. "Really? It's not my job anymore?" I was relieved as my life was filled with school and caring for Dad and Allie. I had no real time to myself.

Miss Anderson said, "Oh no, dear. The judge said that an adult had to be here to care for the baby."

Dad frowned at her.

Her hand flew up to her mouth. "Oh, I'm sorry, Mr. Stroberg. I didn't realize..." her voice trailed off.

He shrugged. "No harm done. But, yes, the court told me that someone had to be here to supervise you both. And Patsy, she'll have dinner ready when I get home from work."

I was delighted.

Well, I was happy at first. Then, Miss Anderson started to act like she was part of the family. She and my dad smiled at each other a lot. My dad seemed a lot happier. I guessed she was his girlfriend. But when she started telling me what to do, as if she were my new mother, I was pretty uncooperative.

"Don't tell me to wash the dishes. You're not my dad. And stop reminding me what time, I need to get to bed!" I was snotty and mean to her, and I was mad at her. I was angry at everyone all of the time. I felt left out.

The truth was, I knew better. One time, I tried to make it right with Miss Anderson. I walked through the park searching for her favorite flower, a trillium. I picked one and brought it back home to her. I even uttered, "I'm sorry for the way I spoke to you."

I saw her eyes well up with tears. "Thanks, Patsy."

I don't know if I caused their breakup or if they did that on their own. However, about a year later, Miss Anderson was out, and a friendly middle-aged woman named Mrs. Smith met me at the door one day after school.

I liked her immediately. She was like my Grandma Davis—kind and warm. She even smelled like Grandma. She was such a cute lady with a wedding ring on her finger.

"Patsy, can you come downstairs and keep an eye on Allie while I take a bath? The tub is all filled up now." I felt my stomach drop. A bath? Memories flooded my thoughts of Mom in the bath for two hours while I would wait at the door for her to come out and notice me. When I got older, I knew I could read three chapters of my book before Mom would be out of the bathroom. The lonely, detached, and impatient pangs of my former life with Mom fought my response. "Well, all right. I am just doing my schoolwork."

After making Allie and me some cocoa, I set up my notebook and history text on the kitchen table. About ten minutes later, she returned.

"Oh, thank you, Patsy! A bath is so refreshing!" Mrs. Smith reappeared with a towel on her head.

"What? You're already finished?"

"Oh, I hope you aren't frustrated?" I stared at her, incredulous.

"No, n-no." I found myself stuttering. "I'll take my books to my room and do my homework there."

"Thanks for helping out. You're a great girl."

Walking up the stairs, I felt a shift in me—an ease with life and a feeling of appreciation. I didn't know ladies could take only ten-minute baths.

Mrs. Smith enjoyed her role in our household. She loved to hear Allie, now five years old, read, especially the back of the Rice Krispies box. He would sound out, "Six little minutes…" as he read the recipe on the box aloud.

"Oh, I just love the way Allie reads that! He's so smart for his age."

She delighted in him. She delighted in me too.

Allie and I would play cards together, and I would read out loud to him. It was easier to be around him now that he was older and went to school. And I liked not having to bathe and feed him, like at first.

A new atmosphere of joy filled our home. Mrs. Smith was kind to me and Allie—the nurturing mother figure I'd not known since I lived with Aunt Gertrude.

A new atmosphere of joy filled our home. Mrs. Smith was kind to me and Allie—the nurturing mother figure I'd not known since I lived with Aunt Gertrude. She always hummed the entire time she cooked. The most savory smells came out of that kitchen. And the meals were well worth the wait. She even ate with us. It was a time of feeling safe and loved.

I looked forward to coming home after school, knowing Mrs. Smith would be there with a snack and a listening ear. Not long after she arrived, I started my period. I told her, "I need, umm, you know—for my period."

"Pads?"

"Yeah. I need that."

"I'll take care of that. I'll get what you need when I go to the store. Don't worry about it. For now, Patsy, I will give you some of mine."

Allie liked Mrs. Smith, and I was comfortable with her. It was a novel feeling to enjoy the attention of such a kind woman. Over time, she started opening up to me. I asked, "Are you married?"

She nodded.

"Why don't you live with your husband, then?"

A sad look came across her face. "Oh, I can't live with him."

"Why not?"

She paused, choosing her words carefully. "My husband is a good man. Deep inside. I used to love him so much when he was young. But now he drinks a lot. And when he gets drunk, he gets mean."

My eyes got wide. "Does he hit you?"

She nodded. "It is good that I can stay here."

"I'm glad you're here with us, Mrs. Smith."

"It is good for me too." She needed a place to stay. And we needed her. We settled into a happy routine.

I turned fourteen and was feeling content with life until one day, I came home from school as usual, and a young man in an Army uniform was standing in the living room next to Mrs. Smith. There was a suitcase on the floor by the door.

I was rattled a little inside, trying to figure out what was happening.

Mrs. Smith looked up at the young soldier with pride in her eyes. "Patsy, this is my son, Jack. He has just returned from serving in the military." I felt scared, and my eyes filled with tears, anticipating what this meant. I didn't like this one bit. The poker in my heart feeling came back.

Jack put his arm around his mother's shoulders. "I'm home. I can take care of her now."

I gasped and tried to hold back my tears. "No! Wait! Are you leaving us?" Tears blurred my vision as Allie locked eyes with mine.

Mrs. Smith put her hands on my face. "I'm so sorry, Patsy. It has been so good to be here. But with my son here, I can return to my home and my life." But she was home. *This* was her home.

"You're leaving right now?" I grabbed Allie's hand and stiffened my stance.

"As soon as your dad comes home from work. I asked him to come home early."

I stood there in shock. No warning. No explanation.

I knew how to be strong, but the ache inside screamed. Allie and I sat together on the couch while awaiting Dad's arrival.

My dad soon appeared, looking as shocked and sad as I did. He nodded to Jack and said, "Thank you for your service." I glared at him and silently pleaded with my dad to fix this. She needed to stay!

"Are you sure you'll be all right?" he asked Mrs. Smith.

"There will be no more problems with my father," Jack said. "Trust me on that."

My dad nodded. There was nothing more to say.

Mrs. Smith kissed Allie on the top of the head and turned to me. "Be good, my little Patsy." And she was gone.

I fell into a depression, having yet another woman abandon me. I coped by reading book after book and writing in my journal. It didn't take Dad long to find another housekeeper, Vicky. This one was young—from the coal fields of Pennsylvania. Allie was afraid of her. I had trained myself not to care. She was unmarried with a one-year-old baby. She needed a place to live, and we needed help, so Vicky and little Annie moved in with us.

Vicky was rough around the edges and mad that her boyfriend, Gene, wouldn't marry her when she got pregnant. They were still in contact. Whenever he called, she'd hang up the phone and say, "Well, that was son-of-a-bitch-n-bastard Gene, giving me a holler." She never called him "Gene." It was always "Son-of-a-bitch-n-bastard Gene sent me a letter" or "Son-of-a-bitch-n-bastard Gene says he'll come to visit us." One day, son-of-a-bitch-n-bastard Gene did just that. He drove from Pennsylvania and packed up Vicky and Annie. When my father came home, I announced we'd lost another housekeeper.

He shook his head. Trying not to be heard, he muttered, "This has got to stop."

18

You Missed Your Chance

It was Easter Sunday, 1955. I was fifteen, and my cousin Marilyn was twelve. We sat beside Aunt Gertrude, and I tried to blend into the wood pew. I wore my best dress to church, hoping no one would notice it wasn't new like the other girls. Agnes and Carol always had new dresses for Easter. I was relieved when we jumped in the car and headed home.

"Are you and your dad coming over for Easter dinner, Pat?"

I shook my head no. "Thank you, Aunt Gertrude, but I have plans this afternoon. And thanks for remembering to call me Pat now."

She smiled, and I couldn't help but feel she was in on some secret. I looked at her with a "What's going on?" expression. She just shrugged and waited until I closed the door.

My dad was reading the paper at the kitchen table. Allie was six years old and playing quietly on the floor with blocks, building a fortress. I said hello and then ran up the stairs to change out of my dress. I put on pants and a top and then bounded back down the stairs. I quickly made myself a sandwich.

"Where are you going, Pat?" my dad asked.

"I'm going over to Carol's. We're going to hang out together at her house. Maybe take a walk or something."

"But your mother is coming today to see you."

I turned slowly. "Mom is coming here? Today?"

He nodded.

"To see me," I said, not as a question but as a challenge.

He nodded again.

I screwed up my face as if I'd just smelled something awful. "Well, I don't want to see *Betty*."

My dad put his paper down and leaned back in his chair. "I should have told you sooner, but I thought—"

"I know what you thought, Dad."

"Look, she's making an effort."

"An effort?" my face reddened. "She lives across town, and I haven't seen her for what? Three years? I was twelve the last time I saw my mother. I am now fifteen! And I'm supposed to drop everything because she is making an effort to come over?"

"Patsy—"

"No, what does she want anyway? There's something in it for her. And remember, Dad, it's Pat now."

"She misses you."

I laughed. "Oh, yes. That's it! Suddenly, after *all* this time, it occurs to her that she has a daughter who she misses."

My dad's face turned stern. "Don't disrespect your mother, Patsy—uh, Pat." He looked at his watch. "She will be here in about a half hour, and I want you to be here."

"I have to?"

"You have to."

Taking my sandwich up to my room, I ate sullenly. I kept looking out the window, knowing she'd walk up the hill any minute. Finally, I saw her turn onto our street. I heard the doorbell ring. I heard Allie running across the floor, squealing with delight. But I wouldn't come out of my room.

"Pat! Your mother is here!" Dad called up the stairs.

What's the use? Let's get this over as quickly as possible. I slowly walked down the stairs.

There she was, clutching her purse in a sky-blue dress and hat. She always said her eyes sparkled when she wore blue. Her perfume filled the air, along with her familiar voice.

She looked at me shyly and said, "Hi, Patsy."

"Don't call me Patsy anymore. It's Pat."

"Well, can we sit together and visit?" she asked my father.

"Oh, yes, of course." Dad guided her into the living room. "Come in and sit down. Pat, pour us some coffee, would you, honey?" My dad sunk into his tan, overstuffed chair while my mother sat on one end of the deep brown sofa. Allie crawled into her lap. I coldly placed their steaming cups of coffee on the side table between them. Patting the other side of the couch, Mom looked at me pleadingly. "Patsy, come sit by me. Let me get a good look at you."

I stood in place. "It's Pat, and um, I didn't know you were coming, Mother—" My dad loudly cleared his throat, signaling me to sit down. "So, I made plans. Sorry." I glanced at Dad as I headed for the front door. As it closed behind me, I said, "I'll be home in time to make dinner." I ran across the yard in fear that someone would come after me.

After that Easter Sunday, my mother showed up at unexpected times. I found it unnerving to have her be there whenever she wanted, with no sense of concern for me. There was never a plan in place, no schedule that I could rely on. Ordinarily, I cooked dinner and included that into my daily routine. But some days, I'd come home from school, and there she would be, cooking in the kitchen, like she belonged there. As far as I was concerned, she didn't.

"We're moving to California," Dad announced at dinner.

"What?" I stared at him in disbelief.

He nodded. "Over the summer. You'll start in a new school next year."

"I just made friends in this *new* school! I don't want to leave my friends!" I was devastated.

"It's already decided, Pat. I'm looking for a new car, and the three of us will drive there."

"Dad! What about Ronnie?" I felt my face turning red at the mention of my new boyfriend. Seeing his lack of surprise, I wondered if he knew where my diary was and had read it.

He sighed while he lit his cigarette. "Pat, please."

I started to cry and got louder, pleading, "I finally have some friends! And I like my school, Dad! Really?"

Allie stopped his building and watched the two of us. It was out of both our characters to fight.

"You'll make new friends, Pat. The schools are new out there. Everything is new in California." I curled up on the couch, pouting as Dad talked on and on about his work options being better in California.

"Why do we have to leave, Dad?" It made no sense to me, this huge move. We didn't know anyone in California. It was across the country! I looked at his face and recognized the look he gets when he's made up his mind. There was no point in trying to change it.

"Pat, the decision has been made. It's time to start a new chapter in our lives."

A new chapter. That made me pause for a moment. A new chapter sounded good to me. While I was still upset about leaving my friends, I saw something positive about the move to California. I could leave my mother behind in Ohio.

I saw something positive about the move to California. I could leave my mother behind in Ohio.

If we moved to California, I could finally be free of her showing up whenever she wanted to, expecting me to be grateful she was there. To not see her again? Now, that bright spot touched a deep part of my soul. I truly despised her. Never seeing her again would make the move worthwhile.

Starting New in California

With mixed emotions, I helped my dad pack up our things and loaded the brand-new blue Mercury for our three-week cross-country adventure. My brother and I took turns riding in the front seat. I was pretty cute in my sleeveless blouse, plaid capris, and matching scarf tied behind my neck. More a tomboy than a lady, I definitely wasn't a kid anymore. In his shorts and short-sleeved knit shirt, Allie was always curious and gathered into his memory many facts about the things he was learning. He wasn't such a bad kid, I had decided. At the ripe age of fifteen, I'd developed some affection for my six-year-old brother.

We stopped at Yellowstone and the four corners. Dad took loads of pictures while Allie and I read, watched for license plates, and played several card games in our car's back seat. Dad even let me drive through part of Wyoming! Burma-Shave billboards placed every few miles teased us with their poems, jokes, and interesting facts, keeping boredom at bay as Dad drove through long stretches of farmland and deserts. I'd started to get excited about what my new life would look like.

We stayed in motels each night, and finally, my dad announced, "We're almost there. Just over those mountains." I was tired of desolate land, straight roads, and sand in all directions, so that was fine with me. "You're going to be surprised at how breathtaking California is."

I laid my head back and closed my eyes. I just wanted out of the car. I must have nodded off because when I opened my eyes, I was surprised at the expanse of greens and browns that spread out before us as we drove further on Route 66.

"Roll down the windows," my dad suggested. A sweet and overwhelming fragrance wafted through the car. "Those are orange trees, you two. We're smelling the blossoms." There were orange groves lining the sides of the highway, filling the air with a beautiful sweetness.

"It is beautiful here!"

My brother and I watched out the window as small towns appeared from the rows of orange and lemon trees as we made our way toward Los Angeles. Before long, we saw the signs of city life with billboards, car lots, higher buildings, more concrete streets, and traffic lights.

"Are we going directly to the rental house?" my brother asked.

"No, we're staying in a hotel one more night."

Allie read the sign, "Welcome to Los Angeles, California! The land of new beginnings."

We stopped at a lookout on one of the small hills. Dad pointed out far-off skyscrapers with bright sun flashing on the windows. "That's where we're heading—downtown Los Angeles." Dad paused. "Yep, this is how I remember it. The best part of Navy life was seeing

California." Allie and I had never seen anything like it. Even though we were tired, we were excited. Dad was studying a map and leaning on the hood of our car. "Okay, you two, I know how to get there now. Get back in the car."

The houses were closer together, and the neighborhoods had palm trees.

"What's that?" Allie asked, pointing out the unreadable letters painted on a wall by a park. We'd never seen gang graffiti before.

"Don't worry about that, Allie," my dad said.

"There's more of those words, Dad."

"There won't be any of that where we will live." When my father spoke in that tone of voice, that meant the conversation was over.

We slowed down due to the traffic but kept getting closer to the skyscrapers. We passed an arch that said "Olvera Street." We saw booths and groups of people taking pictures in a little park. "Food, music, and goods made in Mexico," Allie read aloud. My dad drove in front of a massive building with a large sign: "Union Station." The feeling was magical, and I drank it in.

Driving through a maze of immense and beautiful buildings, Allie and I craned our necks out the window to try and see the tops of the towers. Finally, Dad parked and indicated we should get out. "We're here now, the Hotel Figueroa. Let's head in, kids."

Brightly colored flowers cascaded over the balcony railings. We entered a fancy door into a lobby with exquisite furniture, woodwork, and a black and white floor. It was the tallest building we'd ever been in. I still had that mystical feeling. "Sit here, you two, and wait." I didn't understand, but I knew enough not to ask questions. Dad must have some surprise for us.

"Are we going to see John Wayne?" Allie asked. I nudged him to be quiet.

"Ow," he whined.

"Shh. Just wait and see."

In five minutes, Dad returned, holding the hotel key, and signaled us to follow him. He was so excited. We walked through the big room and up and then down some stairs. Then, we entered an elevator and went to the seventh floor. "Over here, room seven-hundred-and-seven," he said, wearing a big grin. He put the key in the door, opened it, and guided Allie in front of him. I brought up the rear. I was brimming with anticipation. *What is his big surprise?*

Maybe I will like California.

I couldn't see anything ahead with my dad in front of me, so I nearly ran into him when he stopped abruptly. Then I heard Allie exclaim, "Mommy!" His voice rang in my ears like a spear through my heart.

No, it couldn't be. I looked around my father and into the room. Sitting there on the desk chair, dressed to the nines, hair in place, dazzling, and looking like a cat who had swallowed a canary, was my mother.

Allie jumped up and down by her side. "Oh, Mommy's here! Mommy's here!" She looked affectionately at Allie, pulling him close, then turned to face me. "Tell me about your trip, Allie."

I was furious. This! This was why he wanted to move to California? To get my mom away from her family so *they* could start over again? I was dragged away from my friends, Ronnie, Aunt Gertrude, and *my life* so that they could try again.

Betrayed by my father, I couldn't look at him. I was so disgusted. We entered the two-bedroom suite, and she walked toward me as Dad put his hands on Allie's shoulders. I glared at her.

She tried to hug me, and I pulled away. My anger was so great that my words sounded more like growling. "I would have stayed in Ohio if I'd known you were coming out here."

I didn't see it coming. Mom slapped me hard across the face. And before I could think, I hit her right back.

We stared at each other—both in shock. I'm not sure if I was more surprised about my mother hitting me or me hitting her.

"Pat!" my father yelled, stepping in between us.

Shaking with rage, I looked him straight in the eye in defiance. "You lied to me!"

"I did not!"

"Why didn't you tell me she was going to be here? Wait, I know why. Because you knew I wouldn't come if you told me the truth?"

Mom was still rubbing her face, red from the hard slap I had given her. Dad stood silent.

"I-I..." Not knowing how to finish that sentence, I turned on my heels, looking for somewhere to hide. I stomped into the bathroom and slammed the door.

The bond between me and my father cracked. He had been my rock, while my mother had been the source of my deepest pain. But I felt he purposefully tricked me into leaving my friends and family, which stung. I'd trusted him completely, but not anymore. *California. No new chapter for me. It's the same story, just in a different place.*

Is There Hope?

We lived in a rental house on Earle Street in south San Gabriel for almost twelve months. My new school was Mark Keppel High. I made some friends, dated a guy named Tom, and enjoyed a gorgeous magnolia tree that grew right outside my window. The fragrance was intoxicating, and the cooing turtledoves welcomed each morning while the filtered light filled my room.

Mom successfully found us a new, modern, three-bedroom ranch-style home to buy in Covina. It was one of the many houses built across America in the 1950s to house the upswing in families with post-World War II babies. It was bright and affordable, especially for World War II veterans like Dad. He got a special move-in rate and low mortgage—just two hundred and fifty dollars down and payments of seventy-three dollars monthly! Our development in Covina was in the San Gabriel Valley of Southern California, built among the orange groves. The trees were quickly cut down to create even more homes for America's growing families.

The four of us moved into 1324 O'Malley Street, looking in every way to be the "normal" family of two parents and two children. I enrolled in another school—Citrus High School—the fourth school in four years. After a year, the school became a junior college, and I started a fifth school, Covina High, for my senior year. Wherever I was, I tried to make friends, but it was hard. I was always the new girl, shy and the outsider.

The four of us coexisted, none of us happy. I missed Ohio—or perhaps I missed something I never had. Successful in school and finding solace in books and Solitaire, I had moments of teenage pushback toward my parents. Allie seemed most at home in Covina, making friends easily through school and sports.

My mother introduced herself as Mrs. Stroberg to the neighbors. Eventually, it dawned on me that my parents had remarried—somehow, somewhere. But no one told me anything about it. Once again, I was left in the dark with the understanding that I was not to ask for details.

Resentment against my parents grew as I saw that my well-being was never a consideration in their decision-making—individually or together. I was going to turn eighteen in the coming year, and I promised myself I would move out as soon as possible, one way or the other.

In those days, San Gabriel Valley was filled with heavy smog—quite different from today's air pollution. It was a dark orange, brown, and grey, so thick that it sometimes made breathing hard. It was difficult to do outside sports or games due to the sharp chest pains most of us experienced when taking deep breaths. Even though my family lived close to the San Gabriel Mountains, sometimes we couldn't see them. An orange-brown haze settled on the flatlands as far as you could see. When I got home from school in the afternoon, I didn't try to do any outdoor activities. I'd sit on the porch, looking out toward the foothills, feeling sad and lonely.

Inside the house, my mother continued her usual depressed behavior, staying in bed so I'd rarely see her. My brother was around or had friends over to play, but he wasn't a companion due to the age difference. Even though Mom and Allie were home, it felt like I was utterly alone.

One day, I wandered around the house—into one room and the next. Occasionally, I'd walk into my parents' room, look at Mom in bed, say nothing, and then walk out again. After the third or fourth time, Mom asked, "What's wrong?"

I sighed and said, "I'm lonely, that's all."

She looked surprised as if she'd never thought of that before. Studying my face for a few moments, she threw back the covers and swung her legs over the side of the bed. She said, "Come with me."

I followed her down the hall, where she opened a drawer from the built-in and pulled out the game Scrabble. We went into the living room, and she set up the game. At seventeen, this was the first time my mother had ever played with me. I was giddy inside. She was actually spending time with me.

At seventeen, this was the first time my mother had ever played with me. I was giddy inside.

She asked, "Have you played Scrabble before?"

"I watched other people play, but I've never tried. I didn't even know we had that game!"

She smiled. "Well, it's easy. Let's set it up." She explained how each player took seven tiles out of the bag. "See how I set my seven letters on the holder?"

"Right."

"I'll play first, and then you build off of my word, okay?" She started with A D O R E. "Let's see, that'll be five points, then the E is double letter value. So I have seven. And the pink spaces are double word scores."

"So you have fourteen, Mom?"

"That's right. You keep score, honey, okay?"

Gladly, I printed our names in two columns and added her fourteen points. "Okay, here's my word. R E A D. That'll be three plus two is five. And I get a double-word score. So that's ten for me."

From that day forward, she got out of bed when I came home from school. We played Scrabble, and my lifetime of longing for my mother started to lessen as she responded, day after day, to my need for attention. *Is something changing between us?*

But in my heart, I was afraid. *What if I hope, and she disappoints me again?*

When I Marry, My Life Will Be Perfect

Nearly everyone who moved into our neighborhood had little kids—lots and lots of little kids. Allie had plenty of neighborhood friends to play with. But I was one of two teenagers in the entire development.

Fortunately for me, the other teenager, a year older than me, was a tall, handsome Italian boy named Dan. Dan and his siblings lived with their Uncle John and Aunt Rose. And they happened to live right next door. He and I would inevitably meet and spend a lot of time together.

By the time I graduated in the Spring of 1958, Dan and I were officially dating. My parents were not happy about this, especially my dad.

Dad was a stoic Swede who always spoke in an even voice—when he spoke at all. In contrast, Dan's family was big, loud, and proud to be Greek-Italian from Chicago—everything my family was not. I reveled in the noise, the late-night card games, the high-pitched arguments, and the tables filled with endless pasta, wine, and sausages.

While my mother was often in bed, depressed, and unresponsive, Dan's aunt was lively and engaged in raising her sister's children. Dan's family enlisted my babysitting skills and highly developed card-playing expertise. I was welcomed quite often into their home. The closer Dan and I became, the more I spent time at his house.

With his tall stature, dark hair, and charm, Dan oozed sex appeal. He looked like Victor Mature, the Hollywood heartthrob of the day. To my delight, Dan was more than happy to focus his attention on me. I realized for the first time that I had picked up some of my mother's ways. I had an innate awareness of my sexuality. Dan was a wake-up call to my deepest desires—a man with a family that included me. He was a man who made me weak in the knees and who found me irresistible. He was the man who could be my ticket out of my house and the unhappiness of my life.

> *Getting married to Dan would change everything.*

Dan felt the same way I did but for different reasons. He was living with his uncle's family and wanted to be out on his own. Beneath the painful silence at my house and the confusing cacophony at Dan's were two teenagers who wanted nothing more than to get away from their families. We became caught up in the passion of young love. Looking back, I'm not sure we knew anything about love, but we became experts on passion.

It was this shared desperation for escape, added to a highly sexual charge between us, that led Dan to ask me to marry him on Christmas Eve, 1958. I'd found the man of my dreams. I'd never be alone again. Getting married to Dan would change everything.

As Dan and I planned for our future, we both looked for work. Dan found a tradesman job operating machine tools, and LA Die Mold hired me as an office assistant. The Schwarz siblings, Lillian, Bill, Ed, and Jim, owned and ran the company. My boss, Lillian, ran the office while her three brothers oversaw production, molding, and tool making. There were around thirty hourly workers in the production area. I learned basic office procedures, payroll, bookkeeping, and management skills in my four years there. But this job was so much more than employment. Even though I was just a secretary at a company, I experienced family in a way I never had.

First, they were Swedish, and their statures reminded me of the many relatives I'd moved away from in Ohio. But it was more than that. They praised me. So, I worked all the harder and faster. When I left, it took two-and-a-half girls to replace me.

Every day was bookended with at least four people looking me in the eyes and saying, "Good morning," and every afternoon, "Great job today. See you tomorrow, Pat." Never had I experienced such belonging and affirmation.

Bill was the eldest brother, and my desk was just outside his office door. He was the designer and draftsman for the company. He was demanding yet clear about what he needed. Bill was the fatherly one. His tall presence would hover between Lillian's and my desk while he took a coffee and smoke break, and he'd share his opinions and guidance. Their brother Ed was the jokester.

"Pat, you know Tony saw a snake here when emptying the trash last night," Ed said one day. I gullibly looked in and panicked right away.

"What? In here? Ed! Where is the snake now?"

"Quit teasing Pat, Ed. Get back to your office," Bill said.

He winked at me as he walked away, and Lillian reminded me, "You know not to take him seriously, Pat."

He would love to tease me and get me going. Lillian and Bill would fuel his banter or prompt him back to work again and again. I learned how to have a sense of humor and to laugh.

Bill often would sit back in the afternoons and start advising me as an engaged person. One of Bill's soapboxes concerned Dan's work. Unlike my father, who disapproved of Dan and never made any effort to get to know him, Bill went out of his way to chat with him when he came into the South El Monte office at four-thirty to pick me up from work.

One day, Dan arrived early. Bill grabbed Dan and explained how he saw his potential. Bill had explicit opinions about how Dan could work smarter, avoid getting drafted, and shift out of labor as a machinist on the production line to that of a mold maker. They toured the shop while Bill talked, and Dan soaked in the enthusiasm and wisdom of this older man. "Dan, you need to design and create the molds. You'll make more money than you do now. And you can have job security—even in a recession or a war, you'll have job security." Eventually, Dan, so excited about the industry, took his advice and got an apprenticeship just down the street as a mold maker with Bill's connections. He began to earn more money.

Lillian's desk was adjacent to mine. She was constantly mentoring me and throwing me into the deep end. She knew what I didn't, although I was sharp and capable. She was a good teacher, and I was a good student. She helped me speak up for myself by encouraging me to talk back to teasing Bill and all the guys, as well as one hundred and one other lessons. Nestled between these two demanding but kind people, I earned a wage and, more importantly, began filling in many of my childhood holes.

Bill's straightforward commentary about everything, including his sister, startled me. "You know Lillian—she rocks the room with that perfume!"

"Well, Joe, the salesman who comes in each morning, wears a lot of cologne and just about knocks me out," I said.

At that very moment, Joe walked into the office. Bill pointed at me. "She says you stink!" He turned red, and I wanted to fall through the floor. Bill was always stirring up trouble.

On another day, Ed walked in, showing off a five-cent cigar that another salesman had just given him.

"Ed, I'll give you fifty cents not to smoke that cigar!" I said.

They created a light-hearted atmosphere that resulted in high productivity. Clear communication, teamwork, order, humor, and hospitality were infused into my being through this job and the Schwarz family. I was young, in love, and surrounded by people who gave me what I'd always longed for—support, acceptance, hope, and praise. I drank it all in like I was dying of thirst for belonging and stability. And, of course, I was.

Pat's paternal grandparents Alma & Edward Stroberg, with Uncle Ed.

Pat's father Al Stroberg, 1939

Pat's mother Betty, 1930s

Pat at Grandma Davis's, 1942

Pat 3 years old, 1943

Grandma Davis, Betty, Pat, Grandpa Davis, and Aunt Evelyn holding Janny, mid 1940s

Pat, 5, and her mother Betty, 1945

Pat, 6, with Grandma Davis and Marilyn, 3, Pat's cousin

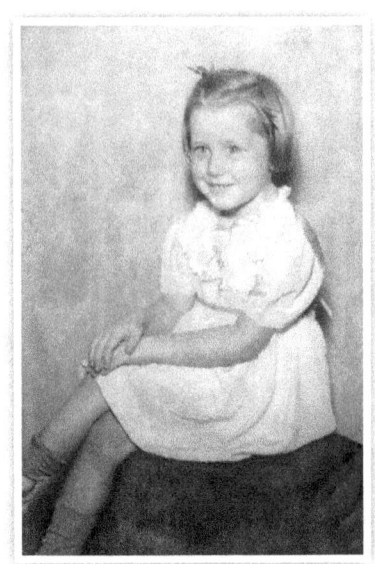

Pat around 1946

Marilyn, 5, and Pat, 8 in 1948

Marilyn and Pat with new baby brother Allie in 1948

Allie and Pat, 1955 cross-country trip

Al (Pat's father) and Allie, 1955 cross-country trip

Al, 1955 cross-country trip

Pat and Allie, Badlands, SD, 1955 cross-country trip

Allie and Pat, Badlands, SD, 1955 cross-country trip

Allie and Pat, Badlands, SD, 1955 cross-country trip

Allie and Pat 1955 cross-country trip

Allie and Pat 1955 cross-country trip

Betty, Pat, Allie, and Al reunited in California, 1956

Pat high school graduation portrait, 1958

Pat and her father Al in 1959

Pat, 20, at LA Die Mold in 1960

Pat's young son Eric, with her mother, grandmother, and father

Pat at Allie's high school graduation in 1966

Pat and Aunt Gertrude on Olivera Street in Los Angeles, 1968

Betty and Aunt Evelyn in 1968

Pat with first husband Dan in 1968

Al with his second wife Alice and dog Shadow in 1972

Pat with husband Bill in 1983

Dr. Gladys, Pat and friend Dorothy

Pat with her dogs Osso and Conrad in 2022

Pat with 102-year-old Dr. Gladys

Who Will Walk Me Down the Aisle?

May 15, 1959: The day had arrived—Dan and I were to be married.

While Dan wouldn't have been my mother's first choice for me, a tender excitement grew between us as we prepared for the wedding. Somehow, she was kind, accommodating, and eager. She helped me choose my dress and find the right kitten heels. She bought Allie and Dad new dress shirts. Of course, she had a new dress, too, in brilliant blue.

Yes, she had broken my heart when I was eleven by leaving me and Dad. I hated her from the day she took Allie and left me behind. The disgust I felt for her intensified when, five years later, she ruined our new beginning in California. But here we were, giggling together and working like a team. She wasn't someone I could count on like I did Lillian, but then again, she was my mother. And beneath my pain was a little girl still crying out for her love.

In a turnabout I couldn't have predicted, Dad was so far away. Always sitting behind a newspaper wall, he felt like a foreigner to me now. Ever since Dan and I got engaged, Dad stopped talking to me. There was, literally, no communication. Instead, there was silence, months of cold silence.

I suppose Dad thought I would change my mind through his silent rejection. Rather, it drove me closer to Dan, who was only too happy to scoop me into his arms as my dad crossed his. I hoped he would soften and come around. For goodness' sake, I was getting married!

Mom and I spent two days clearing out our garage, setting up the chairs and folding tables we borrowed from neighbors and some of Dan's family. Mom ironed the tablecloths and set out the borrowed plates, cups, and champagne glasses. We expected about ten people at the wedding and then back at our house for the reception. The pie, punch, and champagne were all set to be laid out quickly when we arrived after the ceremony. She seemed so levelheaded as I was quiet and apprehensive.

As we readied to leave for the church, Mom ran around in her slip and girdle with a few strategically placed curlers in her hair. "Okay, Allie and Al, we are leaving in forty-five minutes. Let's get Pat to her wedding!"

"Mom, I'm going to wear these earrings after all. What do you think?"

"They're fine, Patsy. See how your brother's doing, okay?" I prodded Allie to the bathroom and maneuvered his cowlick down with Brill cream. Mom met him at the door with his trousers and a new shirt. He groaned but changed without complaint.

I slipped my knee-length dress with the full skirt over my head, careful not to mess up my hairdo. Mom zipped the back and worked on the hook and eye closure. "Patsy, you have the tiniest waist. This dress suits you perfectly. You make a lovely bride."

I checked myself in the hallway mirror. I did look good.

Mom nagged my father. "Al, aren't you getting ready? We're leaving soon." She came up behind me. "Grab a hanky, Pat, and put that lipstick in your handbag."

"Okay, Mom. Take those curlers out here at home. The Aqua Net is on the counter."

We finished our preparation, and the three of us headed to the door. In shock, I looked at my father sitting at the kitchen table. He had made no effort to get dressed—he was still in his khakis and white undershirt. Dad stood up and walked over to me. He held out his right hand, and I took it. "Have a nice life, honey."

Mom grabbed my other hand and guided my devastated frame to the door. "Let's get in the car now, Pat."

In shock, I said nothing. I felt the hot poker burn in my chest. It was the same feeling I felt the day Mom had left with Allie. *This can't be happening!*

I cried the entire drive to the ceremony in Montebello. Arriving at the chapel, I tried to hide my tears. Seeing Dan's Aunt Rose and my friend, Sue, calmed me some. With Mom's direction, they took me straight away to the Women's Lounge to restore my tear-stained face.

And then, I saw Dan chatting with his Uncle Pat through the slightly cracked door of the lounge. My stomach fluttered, and I lost my breath. He looked like a movie star—tall, with dark wavy hair and eyes that held a sensuous smolder. Hearing his voice through the chatter of the room of guests comforted me. Today, I am marrying the most incredible man and will spend the rest of my life with him.

> *Today, I am marrying the most incredible man and will spend the rest of my life with him.*

Entering the small wedding venue, I felt the joy of being Dan's bride. Looking around, I still hoped my father would show up in time to walk me down the aisle as I'd always imagined. My mother whispered something to Allie, and he walked up beside me. Holding his arm out to me, he shrugged and said, "You can't walk down there by yourself."

I nodded, and when the music started, he escorted me down the aisle toward the man who asked me to be his wife. The ceremony was brief. Dan's Greek-Italian family was the inside-out version of my Swedish-Irish family. Their boisterous congratulations overtook our polite smiles and gentle claps. Our new chapter had begun. But I was in tears all the way to the reception.

Returning to our home for the garage reception, Aunt Rose served the pie, and our friend Chris served the punch. Dad was nowhere to be seen. Where was he, and what was he thinking?

There was rice everywhere as we got into the new Buick, loaned to us by Dan's grandfather, to leave for our honeymoon. The toasts, the pie, the gifts were all I could have hoped for. We drove off waving, a young nineteen- and twenty-year-old with no idea what would lie ahead.

And Baby Makes Three

As was common in the 1950s and early 1960s, romance was idealized and promoted as the answer to all life's problems. While madly infatuated with Dan, I had a rather dismal view of marriage. In contrast to my expectations of never being happy, Dan believed in the myth about living happily ever after. These opposing beliefs are what the two of us brought to our marriage.

But as many newlyweds, we spent most of our time in the bedroom, which didn't disappoint. I might not have liked my mother, nor did she assist me in any way during my adolescence. Nevertheless, I was her daughter—sure of myself as a sexual being. And if Dan and I had been able to stay in the bedroom, we'd have had a perfect marriage. But, as we all know, there's much more to life than sex. Once we were dressed and trying to face life together, the disappointments were many and immediate.

Dan was sorely disappointed when our marriage didn't provide the salve to his sense of loneliness or the ecstasy he had anticipated. When being married didn't solve all of his problems, his insecurities still haunted him, and daily struggles continued; he knew exactly who was to blame. Me.

Everything I did and whatever I hadn't done as he desired upset him. He let me know that he was only unhappy because I didn't do what he wanted. He needed to control everything I did so that he could finally feel good about himself. I tried my best but could never please him to the degree he wanted. He became critical of me to the point of obsession.

I tried to keep my temper, but I would wear down, and my anger would show. There was no physical violence, but the emotional cruelty in our loud arguments damaged us both. Dan let me know that being married to me was a massive disappointment to him.

Perhaps another couple might have split up at this point. But we fell into a dangerous cycle of anger and sex. The bigger the fight, the better the sex. It almost became a reward for engaging in so much conflict. Something would set Dan off; he'd criticize me and argue with growing intensity, and we'd find ourselves waking up the following morning after an intense night of lovemaking.

This toxic dynamic intensified Dan's need to control me—fearful that I'd leave him for another man. He wanted to know where I was and who I was with at all times. He falsely accused me of flirting with other men. Consequently, he forbade me from doing anything outside the home without him present. He drove me to work each morning and picked me up every afternoon. I was trapped.

Our big weekly outing together occurred on Sunday afternoons. Dan and I drove to visit our families, who still lived next door to each other. But instead of us all getting together at one house or the other, Dan parked the car and walked to his family's home, and I went to visit my family by myself. Essentially, we all acted as if the wedding never took place. It didn't matter that they'd been neighbors for years and were now in-laws.

My conversations with my parents were friendly after Dad's four months of silence but noticeably absent of any reference to Dan or the state of our new marriage. No one mentioned that my father had refused to attend the wedding. While other young women might turn to their parents for advice at the beginning of a marriage, that topic was taboo for me. So, we chatted about the weather and friends we knew or updates on other family members. My parents and Dan would only see each other if Dan dropped in to say he was ready to leave before I made it over to the house next door.

Granted, neither of my parents was an expert on communicating feelings or resolving conflicts, so even if they had acknowledged their son-in-law, they probably wouldn't have had much helpful advice to give. I suffered severe culture shock. My father was a quiet, withdrawn Swede. Dan was a passionate Italian with a short fuse and loud temper tantrums. I was waking up to the fact that I'd married an emotionally volatile and controlling man and had no one to talk to about my growing despair. My work was busy and gladly distracted me from my circumstances.

A year into our wedded life, Dan proclaimed, "If you don't get pregnant soon, Pat, I am leaving." He wanted me to quit my job, stay home, and raise his children. He had never approved of me working. Even though he was the one who told me to get a job in the first place, he resented that I enjoyed it so much.

My low thyroid and having a tipped uterus worked against our diligent attempts to have a baby. Finally, a missed period. *Now Dan will be happy.* "The doctor confirmed it, Dan. We are finally having a baby!" Elated, we both dreamed of our future family.

> *The doctor confirmed it, Dan. We are finally having a baby!*

I saw blood on my sheets at seven weeks along—a miscarriage. I was devastated. Dan's hopes of marriage transforming his inner pain weren't realized, and my body thwarted our expectation of a baby to complete our family.

While I was hurt, I was not deterred from trying again, and in a few months, I was pregnant for a second time. The joy was short-lived. Another miscarriage. It was a bloody show, flushed down the toilet. I fell into a depression, not only because I'd lost another child but because there was something strangely familiar about the sight and smell of blood. It reminded me of the scenes and odors common in my mother's room when I was growing up. I wondered if my mother had been suffering from miscarriages.

My heart softened a bit toward her. Perhaps this is why she was so depressed, losing one baby after another. Knowing firsthand what that was like, I could identify with her feelings of despondency, failure, and fatigue. *No wonder she had trouble taking care of me—or even staying with my father in the house where she suffered so much loss.* I didn't dare ask her, but I wanted to know if she knew the same grief I was enduring.

Early in 1962, I shared with guarded joy, "Dan, it looks like we are pregnant. Oh, how I hope I don't miscarry." This time, to our delight, I was able to carry the pregnancy to term. As each month progressed, I worried less about miscarrying and more about how I would be as a mother. I had no idea what to expect.

Always the competitive tomboy, I seldom played with dolls. Certainly, my mother was no role model for an adoring maternal figure. What if I didn't bond with my baby? I'd heard some new mothers talk about falling in love with their babies at first sight. But I'd also read about women who sank into deep postpartum depression and had difficulty connecting emotionally with their newborns. What kind of mother would I be?

I found out the answer to that question on August 25th, 1962, at 11:43 p.m. Earlier, with a huge belly, I spent the day reading *Marie*

Antoinette in bed, trying to support my aching back. I called my doctor and described the pain localized in my back. He said that I had Braxton-Hicks, a false labor, so I wasn't particularly concerned. Mom came over with Grandma Davis, helped clean the house, and prepared dinner for Dan and me.

Dan came home after work, and we ate together as usual and then watched TV. My favorite show was about to start at nine o'clock—*Perry Mason*. Suddenly, I felt extremely nauseous and vomited my dinner right there on the floor. I moved to clean myself up, and my water broke onto the bathroom floor. "Dan! Call the doctor!"

Dan called my gynecologist and was so nervous that he hung up on him once the doctor answered. The doctor wasn't fazed by yet another overwhelmed father and called us back. It was time for us to get to the hospital.

Once in the ER, we were instructed to go to the maternity ward down the corridor. I could barely walk and held onto Dan as we slowly moved through the long hall. A nurse came by and asked, "Why are you walking?" She got me a wheelchair, and off we went. Once there, Dan and I went our separate ways. I passed the smoke-filled waiting room and watched Dan join the other soon-to-be fathers, drinking coffee and sharing cigarettes while they worried. I was taken directly to the delivery room.

The doctor said, "You didn't get here a moment too soon, ma'am. The head is crowning!"

There was a large mirror above me, and I could also see the baby's head! I was curious and determined to watch the birth. But a nurse tried to put a mask for gas over my face, and I pushed it away. I said, "I want to see the birth!" She pushed the mask back on my face. I shoved it away again. I wasn't scared, at least not until I heard the screams of a mother delivering in an adjacent room. Finally, the doctor intervened, adjusted the mirror, and I got the best seat in the house to watch the birth of my son, Eric.

When I held my baby in my arms, I felt an intense rush of emotion I'd never felt before or since. I loved this tiny creature and knew

I would do anything, absolutely anything, to protect him. Dan came into the room and grinned.

I looked at him and said, "Let me introduce you to Eric, the light of my life!"

Dan was a proud father, telling anyone who would listen, "It's a boy!"

Seeing Dan's delight and so full of love and gratitude, I had a new hope. *Maybe this is exactly what our marriage needed. We're a family now.*

Broken Hearts Club

While my marriage to Dan was troubled, my parents had set a new record of staying together. From when my mom moved in with us upon our arrival in California in 1955 until my son was born in 1962, my mother lived with my dad and even nurtured us occasionally. Seven years! I was beginning to imagine that my parent's marriage might actually have some semblance of staying power.

But something happened to threaten this precarious equilibrium. With the financial help and insistence of Mom and Aunt Evelyn, my grandparents moved to California from Ohio. They rented a house about twenty minutes away from my parents. At first, I was happy that they were moving closer. I had no way of anticipating the fallout from their decision to leave the Midwest.

Soon after their move, the dynamic between my parents regressed to how it was when I was a child. Mom and Dad started arguing again, with my mother running off to her parents' house when things became too much for her. Once she settled down, she would return to my father and Allie with a grand entrance. The days of drama had returned.

One Sunday, I came for our weekly visit. I walked in and found my dad reading the paper at the kitchen table. "Where's Allie and Mom?" I asked.

He shook his head. "Allie's over at a friend's house. Your mom? Your guess is as good as mine."

I stood awkwardly for a moment, wanting to sit down and talk with my father but not knowing if I would be welcome. He must have picked up on my feelings. "Want a cup of coffee, Pat?"

I sat down at the table. "That would be great, Dad."

He poured two cups, lit his cigarette, and sat down with me.

"I hope you don't mind me asking about…" My voice trailed off.

Dad smiled sadly. He looked at me, and I could see him weighing whether to talk to me as his child or another adult. He must have needed an ally in this messy situation, and I was the closest thing to a confidant he could find. The adult conversation won. "You're a married woman now, Pat."

I was surprised that he acknowledged that. I ventured forward carefully. "Allie told me Mom has been moving back and forth between here and Grandma and Grandpa Roy's."

Dad smiled sadly. He looked at me, and I could see him weighing whether to talk to me as his child or another adult.

He looked away, his eyes full of memories. "I was afraid this would happen."

"What do you mean?"

He sighed, and smoke billowed from his nose and mouth. He finally looked at me again.

"Why, Dad?" I asked while hugging my mug, gaining the strength to listen to his response.

"I've always believed that the problems your mother and I have had were made all the worse by your grandparents. You know, there's an emptiness inside of her, Pat. She is never happy. And she's so upset that our marriage doesn't fill her up."

"Yep, Dad. You're right. You know, I feel that happens with Dan too. He blames me for whatever negative things he feels." I felt my face turn red, and the ache in my gut increased.

Dad shook his head, and there was a quiver in his voice. "I'm so sorry, Pat. I was hoping against hope that it would be different for you." I felt his unspoken tenderness toward me. He felt my pain. He knew what I was going through.

I caught a glimpse of what my father had felt about me marrying Dan. Would I have listened to him if he'd talked to me before the wedding? I don't know. I never will. We both sipped our coffees as though it could provide the help and comfort we both longed for.

He broke the silence. "When your mother had nowhere else to go, she stayed with us. In her way, she tried to work things out with me." I agreed, seeing that there had been more interaction these last few years. "But now that she has an easy escape route to her parents, she leaves at the slightest provocation. She goes to avoid further struggle. Grandma and Grandpa Roy fill her head with self-doubt like they did when you were a baby."

"She gives up on the marriage?" I shook my head, sickened by the pattern.

"I'm afraid so."

I nodded. "I can see it, Dad." We sat in silence as I looked back on my life. "Is that why she left me with Aunt Gertrude while you were in the war?"

"Yes. Your mom had no faith in herself as a mother, so she left you with Aunt Gertrude."

Pieces of the puzzle fit together in my mind.

I took a deep breath, feeling the hot poker of rejection again. "I always wondered why she wasn't around. No one's ever talked about it, and I didn't know how to ask."

"We should have told you something, honey, especially when you got older. But I didn't know how to bring it up, and I just didn't want to say anything bad about your mom."

I laughed. "You didn't have to, Dad. She's done enough on her own to break my heart."

Dad blinked, recognizing the damage she had caused. "Getting us away from your grandparents was one of the main reasons I moved us all out to California. I hoped that if we made a clean break from them, your mother and I would have a better chance."

"And it worked for a while."

He nodded and sighed. "Quite a while. And now, they're here."

"Has she moved out for good?"

"I don't know. I hope not."

I paused and let it sink in—my mother had made and continued to make significant changes in her life that were detrimental to me and Allie without considering us. "I hope for Allie's sake she stays here, Dad. He is a sixteen-year-old kid. He needs a mom."

You Will Do the Right Thing

I sat at the kitchen table while Grandma Davis bathed Eric in the kitchen sink. I'd never seen my grandmother so happy. She giggled as Eric played and splashed in the warm water. She kissed him on the head and then turned to me. "I am falling in love all over again!"

I laughed. "Again?"

"Oh yes, Patsy. I felt the same way when you were small."

That bewildered me. *Has anyone ever loved me that way?*

After his bath, we put Eric down for a nap and played cards at the kitchen table. After a while, I looked up at Grandma Davis and asked a question I'd had on my mind for some time. "What was I like when I was little? Mom said I was a difficult child."

She looked up with a crinkly smile. "Oh, you were the light in my heart, dear Patsy. You were a lively one but not any more difficult than any other *normal* baby. Your mother, though—you know I love my daughter, Pat, but she was a difficult child. Believe me. Your Aunt Evelyn has always been responsible, quiet, and good in school. But from the moment Betty was born, she was a handful. Mood swings, the likes I'd never seen."

"Wasn't it hard for you all during the Depression?" I wanted to know more about my family, especially my mother's childhood.

Sadness spread across Grandma's face. "The Great Depression was horrible. Roy lost his job. We couldn't pay rent. At one point, we were homeless, living in a tent Roy put together with things people had thrown away. We stood in those bread lines for hours, which was very hard on Betty and Evelyn. Sometimes, the food ran out before we made it to the front of the line." Her eyes filled with tears. "It's hard to even think about my two girls going hungry, living in the cold."

"I'm sorry, Grandma." I felt guilty. "Let's talk about something else. I just wanted to understand my mother better."

Patting her eyes dry, Grandma said, "Oh, I understand. I think it's time you knew more about what happened. Even though your mother was twenty, she wasn't ready for marriage or motherhood. We were so poor.

"Your father's gas station was near where we lived. Al was a handsome man, nine years older than she was. And financially stable. He gave her a job at the gas station. She was such a pretty little thing. He fell for her right away. I'm not sure if she ever truly loved your dad, but when he asked her to marry him, she knew he could take care of her. He could provide the kind of security she'd not known."

I took this in with sadness, knowing that my dad had always loved her, and she said yes to his proposal for security. But I also had a sense of understanding. She'd known homelessness and hunger. It was just that heartbreak had been the result.

Grandma continued. "They married, and she got pregnant right away. I was delighted to have my first grandchild. But everything about becoming a mother was hard on her. We didn't know what to call it back then, but Betty suffered from—what's the name of that condition?"

"Postpartum depression?"

"Yes, that's it. And she had it bad. Your father worked long hours at the gas station, and she sank into a very dark place. I came over often to see you both. You were such a gorgeous baby with golden hair. You were interested in everything. Bright blue eyes—I knew you were smart the moment I first laid eyes on you. But..." She stopped.

"But what?" I asked nervously. "Was I truly awful?"

With a huff, Grandma Davis said, "Absolutely not! It was not your fault." Her eyes looked out the window, but I could tell she wasn't seeing the flowers and lawn outside. She was caught up in a vision of the past. I waited.

Grandma set her cards on her lap and looked deeply into my eyes. "Patsy, I did the best I could for you. Or at least I tried. But it was simply too much for her."

"*I* was too much for her?" I felt my hands tremble.

She smiled sadly. "Having a baby who needed her and everything that accompanies it, my dear. Do you remember how your mother spent so much time in bed?"

I nodded.

"Serious depression and some other, well, illnesses." Her eyes got a little wet again. "Oh, dear, I remember before your dad left for the war, he would be at work, and I'd come over to see you and Betty. I could hear you crying before I even got up to the porch.

"I'd go inside and find you in your crib, red in the face, screaming so loudly. Hungry, with a wet diaper. After I got you cleaned up, I'd go find Betty, who was either asleep in bed or sitting in a chair staring off into space. It was like she couldn't hear you.

"I'd say to her, 'Betty, what's wrong with you? Don't you hear Patsy crying?' She would look at me with a dazed expression.

"'Oh,' she'd say. 'Was she crying?'

"I would put you in her arms. 'Now feed her, Betty. I won't leave until you take care of your child.'"

A jolt of anger shot through me. "I can't imagine letting Eric go hungry or wearing a dirty diaper."

"Of course not, my dear Patsy. You have the heart of a mother, although you never got that from yours. When your dad left for the war, we feared for your safety. That's why we all agreed that Gertrude would be the best person to care for you. She was so good with children, and Betty couldn't do it. You know that more than anyone, Pat. Your mother has so many burdens that she doesn't think about others. About you. About Allie."

Grandma Davis looked at me intensely. "But it wasn't your fault, Pat. Don't ever think that it was."

I asked my mother to come over to my house the next day. She wasn't keen on it, but I pressured her, and she relented. Showing the signs of middle age, wearing fifteen extra pounds and a blue shirt matching her eyes, Mom arrived about half an hour late and grabbed a chair at the kitchen table.

"Want some coffee?"

"Yes, that would be nice."

After I put a hot cup in front of her, I sat down and took a deep breath. However, before I could say anything, Mom said, "Don't start with me, Pat."

Having heard how she treated me as a baby, I decided to be honest with her. "Mom, listen to me. You really must move back in with Dad and Allie."

"And now you're the expert on marriage? You've been married how long now?"

"That's not the point. Allie needs you."

A frown crossed her face. "But Pat, you know how your father is. So boring, it's painful."

"Allie's a teenager. You're his mom."

"Not an ounce of passion in him. How can I possibly bear it?" She looked toward the door longingly.

I felt a ripple of anger flow through my body, but I kept my voice steady. "You *will* bear it because you are Allie's mother. Your feelings about Dad aren't important. It's not about Dad or you. Allie needs you to be there for him until he graduates high school."

My mother's eyes flashed with annoyance. "But, Pat, that's three years from now!"

"Yes, Mom. Yes, he graduates in 1966, and you will be Allie's mother for the next three years."

"Don't talk to me that way," she snapped, smoothing her hair. "Of course, I'll be his mother for the next three years. It doesn't matter where I live."

I glared at her, fighting the desire to unleash years of pain and fury in her direction. "I am not going to let you off the hook. You weren't there for me, but you will be there for him. He needs you to be a mom who lives with him, is there for him every morning when he leaves for school, and greets him every afternoon when he returns. Every single day. And when he walks through graduation and gets his diploma, you will be there to celebrate with him. Let me repeat. It's not about *you*, Mom. It's about your child, Allie, and what he needs."

She frowned as if something extreme was being asked of her. "Three years?"

I nodded and stared her in the eye. "Every day."

She leaned back in the chair, momentarily lost in her thoughts. Her shoulders slumped as if defeated. "Okay, I'll move back in with them. But I'm staying in your old room, and the moment Allie graduates, I'm out of that house."

She got up and walked out the door, her hot coffee still on the table.

Amazing Grace

When Eric was born, I left my job at LA Die Mold. Lillian had mentored and mothered me, supplementing what I hadn't received from Mom. So, with tears in my eyes, I said goodbye to my second family and became a full-time homemaker.

As was common in the sixties, we had one car, and Dan took it to work each day, leaving me homebound. He refused to let me leave our home to take classes, constantly worrying men would pursue me or that I would become too smart. I found myself talking a lot with my neighbor, Sophie, who was stranded in the same way, only she sold Tupperware in the evenings. Beyond our chatting, our excitement was the daily bread truck, a standard neighborhood service back then. Driving slowly and playing a tune through the neighborhood, the truck would stop when people would come out of their homes. The large side-by-side back doors opened wide, and cigarettes, basic food staples, and treats were displayed and ready for us to buy.

I started smoking when I was fourteen to fit in with the crowd. By the time I was working full-time at LA Die Mold, I was going through three packs of Marlboros a day. Dan smoked at least that much. I cut back when Eric was born, making sure to never smoke around him. The bread truck was my cigarette source, charging twenty-five cents a pack. It was an expensive habit. And then, Sal, the driver, raised his prices one day to thirty-five cents a pack. I had to walk back to the house to get the dime. I was mad but bought them anyway. By the time I was home and lighting up, my Irish temper was flaring. Furious, I lit the cigarette, tapped the burning ember into the ashtray, and put it back in the pack, leaving it for Dan. I never smoked again.

While visiting with Sophie one afternoon, I said, "I can't take doing nothing all day." Sophie completely understood. So she and I decided that if we couldn't leave home and learn new skills or ideas, we'd study things together that interested us both. We liked reading and were hungry to find a purpose beyond cleaning the house and cooking dinner. We walked, with our children in tow, to the park daily. We'd stop at the library occasionally, finding books, magazines, and audio tapes to check out. We sifted through these new ideas, facts, and philosophies at the playground, in each other's kitchens, and while taking walks. Our shared appetite for knowledge was a life-saver for me—Sophie too. We dove into our studies with enthusiasm.

I discovered that I had an insatiable desire to understand how the world worked. There was so much that triggered my curiosity. Growing up, little to nothing was explained to me, and I'd never had the chance to address my many traumatic experiences. I had a myriad of questions. *Why do I feel the way I do? What did I do to make my mother reject me? Why didn't Dad come to my wedding?* And so many more.

We studied various topics from different viewpoints, including world religions, self-help, psychology, astrology, dream interpretation, spirituality, natural medicine, and alternative health ideas. I had a sense of myself as a spiritual being, having believed in the existence of God since I was a child. Paying greater attention to dreams and things unseen, I now had an undeniable sense that I had been cared for at critical times in my life, and perhaps an angel was sitting on my shoulder.

But I also needed to explore other ways of seeing the world. I felt it was important for us to question what our families, culture, and religion taught us. We needed to decide for ourselves what we would believe. During this time, I studied the writings of Edgar Cayce, who has been called the father of the New Age movement. Breaking out of the narrow worldview my family had given me was liberating. I was open to learning, and I soaked up all I could. My personal spiritual journey became woven into every aspect of my life.

However, Dan liked me isolated. "Pat, did you two take the children to the library again? Wish you'd stay put."

"But Dan, I need to get out of the house. I get stir-crazy. The library had a panel of three veterans speaking today. It was great."

He just frowned.

I loved being Eric's mom, but I missed going to work. I longed for the interactions Lillian, her brothers, and I had shared. My mind needed a challenge, and I was so eager to grow. Reading and studying helped me find a worldview of my own.

> *I now had an undeniable sense that I had been cared for at critical times in my life, and perhaps an angel was sitting on my shoulder.*

Sometimes, I would bicker with Dan when he tried to limit my activities, question my thoughts, or silence Sophie and me. I learned to watch my words and be strategic with my time. I didn't want to set off his loud rants and cruel put-downs about me and the things that made me feel alive. Washing the dinner dishes was better than sitting near him. I couldn't stand to be in the same room with him. Often, I was reduced to tears and desired to escape. I was fearful to drink alcohol because if I relaxed, he'd surely attack me with his vicious words. My mind filled with knowledge and perspective while my heart was held captive and crushed.

I wanted to raise Eric with a moral foundation—a religious tradition that would give him a framework for finding purpose in his life. I'd been raised in the Lutheran church, and Dan was Catholic. When I approached Dan about attending church, he wasn't interested.

"If it's not important to you," I insisted, "I'll take Eric to the Lutheran church with me."

That triggered an immediate and angry reaction. "You will not take him to a Lutheran church! My son will be raised Catholic, and that's final!" There was to be no further discussion. I was relieved, honestly, that he didn't forbid me to attend church without him, seeing how jealous he was. So, I contacted the local parish and converted to Catholicism.

Once I completed catechism classes, I brought Eric with me to mass. Initially, I thought I was doing it primarily for his sake. But the more I attended, the liturgy fed a deep need in my heart and a sense of God's presence in my life. I began keeping track of the spiritual moments in my daily journaling, noting when I felt an angel was with me. As I continued to read other types of spiritual materials, I created a worldview that was unique to me.

Sophie and I continued taking our children to the park and talking through our discoveries about our spiritual paths. "Sophie, I consider myself 'eclectic' and suspect many people feel the same. I gather information and insights from various sources to find what works for me." She nodded in agreement.

"Amazing Grace" was my favorite hymn. The tune, the history of its writing by John Newton, and the message of God's loving grace resonated deeply within me. When I complained to the choir director that it wasn't sung enough, he challenged me. "You want to sing 'Amazing Grace'? Then join the parish choir."

And so, I did. But the choir director never chose it as one of our songs. One day after church, one of the priests greeted me and asked me how I was doing. I said it would be much better if the choir director would have us sing "Amazing Grace"! And I filled him in on the reason I joined the choir.

He smiled and said, "Let me take care of it."

The following week and most of the weeks afterward, we sang "Amazing Grace." As Aunt Gertrude once said, "Always go to the top if you need something done."

To this day, each time I sing this song, I experience the truth of what Edgar Cayce wrote: "If you learn music, you'll learn most all there is to know." God's grace and love became foundational for me. It was a support under my feet, a much-needed comfort, and a purpose when life didn't happen as expected.

My mom and Dan seemed to force the unexpected into my world again and again.

Pork Chops on the Stove Again

When Eric was around three, I called Grandma Davis to see if she wanted me to bring him over for a visit. The phone rang and rang. It worried me because I was reasonably sure she and Grandpa Roy were home. After several rings, I hung up, wondering if I should go over to check on her.

About an hour later, my mother called. "Pat, Grandma fell getting out of the tub and trying to answer the telephone." I was horrified. *My phone call?*

"Is she okay?"

"Not really. The ambulance just left to take her to the hospital. The medic said it looks like she broke her hip."

"Oh, no! Which hospital?"

Mom told me, and I said, "I'll meet you there."

Driving to the old neighborhood, I left Eric with Dan's Aunt Rose, and then I met Mom and Grandpa Roy at the ER in Arcadia. The hospital staff told us that Grandma's hip was broken and she would need surgery as soon as possible. I stayed at the hospital for as long as possible, knowing Dan would expect his dinner on time as usual. I returned to Covina and then kept in touch with Mom and the hospital by phone. I was told the surgery was successful and I could visit the next day.

But when I entered Grandma's hospital room the following morning, she complained of great pain. She was also running a high temperature. The doctor visited while I was in the room, and he had a stern look on his face. To the nurse, he said, "She needs a blood test. Get a sample and take it to the lab ASAP."

A few hours later, the doctor told us that Grandma had contracted a staph infection in her hip joint. She was given high-strength antibiotics, but it took days to get the infection under control. As a result of this infection, her hip was pushed out of its socket, and she never fully recovered. From that day forward, she had to rely on a walker to get across the room. Her days of pain-free movement were over.

Seeing my tiny Grandma Davis in the hospital, I recalled how loving she was to me as a little girl, snuggling with her, engulfed in her fur coat, and her reading aloud to me. How, with no more than a third-grade education, she managed to raise two daughters through the Depression and work as a maid was beyond me. Watching Mom wrangle Grandpa Roy, and being sweet and attentive to Grandma after surgery, I felt proud to be in their family line.

However, every time I saw her struggling with her walker, I felt a pang of guilt. My phone call caused her to hurry out of her bath and fall. I felt responsible for her unending disability.

On a Friday evening in June of 1966, we celebrated Allie's graduation from Northview High School. Dan wasn't interested in attending, so I drove to my parents' place and went with them. Dad had dropped Allie off earlier so he could put on his cap and gown. The high school was close, and I didn't think anything of the fact that my parents didn't say much to each other. We found Grandpa Roy, and Grandma Davis, and I helped her navigate the stairs with her walker. Allie beamed. I was so proud of him and Mom. She had kept her promise.

The next day, Allie called me. "Pat, she's gone."

"Who's gone?" My stomach lurched.

"I went out last night with some friends and got home late, so I slept in this morning. When I got up, I saw Mom had packed up all of her things and left."

I let out a huge sigh. "I can't believe it. After all of the times she has left, I don't know why it surprises me this time."

"At least you got her to stay here until I graduated. But, boy, she didn't stay a minute more than she had to."

"I'm sorry, Allie. You know it's not because of you."

"It's not your fault, Pat."

"I wish you'd had a brother. He would know how to help you at a time like this."

Allie was silent for a moment. "I didn't need a brother. Pat, you've been a good sister. What I needed was a mom I could count on."

I didn't know what else to say. We both knew that no matter what our mother said or did, we'd never be able to rely on her.

"And guess what she left on the stove?"

"No! Not pork chops and potatoes!"

"That's right." Exasperated, we both laughed for a second.

> *Pat, you've been a good sister. What I needed was a mom I could count on.*

"Well, I guess that's one consistent thing Mom does," I said. "When she leaves us, there's always pork chops and potatoes."

Allie sighed. "I hate pork chops."

Sunday, two weeks later, I got another call from Allie. "Pat! There's a woman living in the house!"

"What house?"

"Our house. You know Mom's living at Grandma and Grandpa's, and this lady, Alice, showed up yesterday."

I was flabbergasted. "Well, where did this lady come from? When did Dad meet her? *Where* did Dad meet her?"

"I have no idea. She showed up early in the morning, waking me up. Dad came out of his room dressed for the day, quickly introduced her, and then they left.

"I had no idea what was going on, so I went ahead and hung out with my friends. When I got home, no one was there. I stayed up late watching *The Tonight Show,* and in they walked. This time, Alice had a suitcase."

"She moved in? Into my old room?"

"No. Into Dad's room!"

"He's got a girlfriend? He's living with a woman—with you in the house?"

He paused for a moment for dramatic effect. "Oh no! They're not living together."

"They're sharing the same room and the same bed. What would you call it?" I was confused.

"I would call it *being married*."

I gasped. That was more than I could take in. My father, Albert Stroberg—stable, long-suffering, devoted husband, faithful to my mother through years of betrayal—is married to another woman?

"You're speechless, aren't you? So, Dad walked up to me and stood in front of the television."

"He did? And…?"

"And he announced, 'Allie, Alice and I got married today in Las Vegas!' But can you believe he's married to someone other than Mom?"

I calculated what this meant. "Then Dad and Mom must have gotten divorced—again!"

Allie sighed. "Well, that's assuming they remarried when we came to California!"

I chuckled. "Do you think Mom and Dad lived together without being married?"

"Regardless of the details, he sure didn't wait long, did he?"

"A couple of hours!" We both started laughing at the absurdity.

"What is she like?"

"Hard to say. I haven't talked to her yet."

It hit me like a ton of bricks. "This must be so awful for you, Allie. To be there, with her, with them, as a *couple*! Are you okay?" I was worried about my little brother.

"I guess so. I don't really know what to think."

"I'm going to talk to Dad tomorrow. This was not the way to deal with this. We should have gotten the chance to meet her in advance." It was odd for me to feel angry at my father these days. After our recent conversations, I thought he would confide in me about something this important. I felt left out once again.

"I can't wait to get out of this house. I'm glad I'm leaving for college at the end of the summer."

"I'm glad for you, too, Allie. I am."

I Married My Mother

I brought six-year-old Eric to visit Mom and my grandparents on Christmas Eve that same year. As I walked into the house, Grandpa Roy was sitting in the living room, complaining of feeling weak and short of breath. Mom stood over him and said, "Dad, we need to get you to the hospital!"

"I'm not going to the hospital! No reason to cause a big fuss!" He turned his head away angrily.

"Grandpa, tell me what you're feeling."

He waved me away. "It's nothing, Pat. Just feeling off a bit."

Grandma came out of the bedroom with some fresh clothes. "Roy, you know the only reason you don't want to go to the hospital is that you have a hole in your underwear. Now, put these fresh clothes on while Betty calls for an ambulance."

Grandpa Roy stood up slowly. "You women!" and then carefully made his way to the bathroom, grabbing the clothes from his wife as he passed by. Mom picked up the phone and dialed for help. She'd just put the receiver down when we all heard a thump.

"Roy!" Grandma called out.

Mom immediately sprinted to the bathroom. Slowly opening the door, she saw Grandpa slumped against the wall, still sitting on the toilet with his underwear down around his ankles. "Dad!" Mom cried and ran to his side.

The ambulance arrived quickly. The medics began CPR and then took Grandpa Roy away on a stretcher. I couldn't tell if he was alive or dead. We followed the ambulance to the hospital. Once in the emergency room, we were told that Grandpa Roy had passed away.

Perhaps it was just a coincidence, but Grandpa Roy's death in 1967 seemed to trigger a noteworthy reorganization within my family. Aunt Evelyn and her husband, Bill, left Ohio and moved about an hour and a half south of us to Escondido. They wanted to leave the snowy winters behind, be able to visit their son, Roy, who was stationed in San Diego, and still be close enough to those of us up in Los Angeles County.

I enjoyed Bill, a kind man who liked building furniture in his garage. Evelyn treated him poorly, as she did almost everyone else, and I wished Bill would stand up for himself. But it was nice to have more of the Ohio family close by.

With Grandpa gone and Grandma Davis dealing with her disability, it wasn't safe for her to live alone. Mom sold her parents' house and bought an apartment in Long Beach, but Mom didn't want Grandma Davis living with her full time—no one wanted that. So, we came up with a solution. Mom, Aunt Evelyn, and I passed Grandma between our homes. She was a nomad, living with each of us for several months at a time. When Grandma's nonstop chattering began making our ears tired, we were ready to move her on to the next house. My home was located in between Aunt Evelyn's and Mom's houses, so it often served as the "handing off" location when easygoing but needy Grandma Davis would go from one place to the other.

Dan's side of the family had conflict and tension, and so did mine. At first, to keep drama to a minimum, we had to do two of everything—two Thanksgivings, Christmases, and birthday parties. It was exhausting, but we both wanted these eventful times with our families. After many tiring years of hosting double celebrations, I hit my limit. Boldly, I invited everyone to the same Thanksgiving dinner. I made it clear: "We really want you here. If you don't want to come, though, okay."

I soon realized that simultaneously having everyone at our home was also challenging. Two people stood out among the others—the stars of the show, so to speak.

Dan was the leading man. He wasn't just big; he was bigger than life. Loud, self-obsessed, and bursting with sexual charisma, Dan commanded everyone's attention. As his wife, one might have assumed I would be his counterpart, but no. The starring lady was my mother. On the regular, while the rest of us simply walked into a room, both Dan and Mom made *an entrance*.

And what an entrance Mom made. Men stared, and women glared when my mom showed up. Her laugh was contagious, her smile captivating, and she created an irresistible vortex that drew people toward her.

But my mother was demanding if she didn't receive the proper attention she required. So, she got attention one way or the other. Whether she was happy or upset, she created chaos wherever she went. There was nothing calming or soothing about Mom. She was either turned on brightly like a strobe light or curiously dark, trapped inside her thoughts and sufferings. But regardless of mood, she would not be overlooked or dismissed.

> *While the rest of us simply walked into a room, both Dan and Mom made an entrance.*

While I refer to Dan and Mom as the stars of the show, I don't mean to imply that they were starring in the *same* movie. No, they saw themselves as the center of their universe and competed with each other for center stage. Both powerful in their own right, they often collided and created more than enough collateral damage on the rest of us trying to enjoy some pie or open a Christmas present or two.

It was Christmas Day 1968. Dan and I expected eighteen for the midday meal. Opening a tube of Ritz crackers and eating a stack of them, Dan asked, "Pat, when are people coming again?"

"For the tenth time, Dan, three p.m.! Now, can you get those folding chairs like I asked you?"

"It's almost game halftime. I'll go out to the garage then."

I knew I was on edge, having his and my sides together. But the house looked festive. We were ready, and it would be a great day if Dan kept his cool.

I was fussing about basting the ham and peeling potatoes when Mom let herself in through the patio door. "Mom! You're here already?"

"Hi, Patsy. I couldn't remember the time you said to come. I brought mashed potatoes."

Holding the seventh potato mid-peel, I regulated my voice. "Mom, I'm making the mashed potatoes; you were supposed to bring green bean casserole and a pumpkin pie. And you're an hour and a half early."

"Oh, honey, we'll make do with what we have. I'll just go sit in the garden and keep the dogs occupied."

"Of course, you're not even offering to help," I mumbled beneath my breath. "Okay, Mom. Thanks. Glad you're here." I knew not to confront her, have Eric play a game with her, or even give her a chore. None of us wanted to hear her whine or feel the weight of her pouting if she was set off. She grabbed a deck of cards from the kitchen drawer and played Solitaire on the patio until Dan's Aunt Rose and Uncle John arrived at three.

In a state of shock, I sat in my chair at the head of the long table as the dinner, conversation, and passing of the plates went on around me. *I married my mother.* The similarities were so obvious, yet I was only seeing it now. Dan put himself first. My mother did as well. He dismissed my concerns, and she seemed unaware and certainly non-responsive to my needs. They were both erratic, self-absorbed, reactive, and unable to make room for anyone but themselves.

Dad sat near Dan at the other end of the table. Alongside him was Alice, his wife. They both quietly tolerated the noise and loud conversations. My dad had finally married a faithful woman, albeit anxious and insecure. It was easy to like Alice. She gave me no reason to dislike her beyond the initial shock of her presence in my family home. Alice was a small, round, perfectly groomed woman who dyed her hair red, trying to make the most of what she had to work with. I suspect she was intimidated by my mother, having no chance to match her beauty or craziness. But then again, maybe she wasn't.

My father loved Alice, and any feelings he had about my mother, positive or negative, were never expressed. He seemed content with her, a woman who would never cause a scene or call attention to herself. I looked at them and felt such a kindred spirit with my father—a shared pain that cut into my heart.

Even though he was happy with Alice at this point in his life, he and I had made the same poor choice with our first mates. I harbored a deep sadness and resentment toward Dad for not attending my wedding. But suddenly, I saw the situation more clearly.

On our wedding day, Dad knew I was making the same mistake with Dan that he made with Mom. That was why he was so distressed when I married him. After eighteen years of confusion, I forgave Dad instantly. I now admired how he wanted to protect me from choosing a similar life of pain and betrayal. Words he never spoke would have helped.

Dad finally got free of Mom and had a quiet, comfortable relationship with Alice. I looked at Dan and realized I was still in a dangerous situation. No one had hurt me more than Mom. And I was yet to discover that Dan would ultimately come in a close second.

Mom, I See What They Do to You

For the next several years, we settled into a routine. We met at my house to hand Grandma off, so Mom, Aunt Evelyn, and Grandma Davis became regular visitors to my home. While I had been around these three women as a child, this was my first glimpse into their relationships with each other from an adult perspective. Mom's talent at creating chaos, my Aunt Evelyn's jealousy about how others tolerated her antics, and Grandma's acquiescence to both became all the more apparent to me.

Perhaps it was the jarring loss of her father or some other issue I knew nothing about, but once my mother moved to Long Beach, she wanted to have fun. Doing this, she gave in to two addictions—drink and food. She gained weight at a steady pace, reaching about two hundred and fifty pounds before she leveled off.

But nothing stood between Mom and her social life—not drinking, not her weight, and not even the fact that she had her mother living with her for long periods of time. She knew men and how to manage them. My mom gathered stray men in the same way that some pick up stray dogs. At any weight, Mom was engaging and hard to resist.

When the family got together, Mom usually brought her current rescue boyfriend, of which there were many. No one said anything about it except Aunt Evelyn, who often seethed with jealousy, even though she was married to Bill, a kind and loving man who deferred to her dominance.

The first one who stayed long enough for me to remember was Ed—a skinny man with a lost puppy dog face. Unable to sustain an adult relationship, he followed my mother around in hopes of a crumb of attention. As a recovering alcoholic, he got uncomfortable when wine or after-dinner drinks were served. He especially didn't like Mom drinking, as it made it all the harder for him to resist joining in. Ed was soon replaced, much to our shared relief.

In the same way that others picked up stray dogs, my mom gathered stray men.

The next man of note was a short Italian named Johnny. I didn't particularly like him because he was so clingy and possessive. Mom would hide in the bathroom to get distance from him, taking baths for up to two hours. He didn't much like Mom's drinking either. She told me that they had gone shopping at the grocery store, and she put a bottle of wine into the basket. Johnny put it back on the shelf. Mom put it back in the cart. He put it back on the shelf. She put it back in the cart. Eventually, she won, of course. She ultimately got her way.

Mom and Johnny came over for dinner one night and pulled me aside. Johnny handed me several pieces of paper stapled together.

"What's this?" I asked.

"Your mother has agreed to marry me."

"What?" I looked at her with surprise.

She shrugged like it was no big deal. I looked down at the papers. It was a long list of items—couch, silverware, car, etc.

"What's all of this?"

"Oh, Pat, it's a list of everything we own. A list for him and a list for me."

Johnny nodded. "That's right, Pat. You know, we've both been married before. We're not new to this..." he waved his hand as if pointing toward marriage as a location.

Mom interrupted. "If the marriage doesn't work out, we'll already know what belongs to who, and it won't be so..." She couldn't think of the word.

"So if you get a divorce, you'll already have the assets sorted out. Sort of like a prenuptial agreement?"

Johnny clapped his hands with a big smile. "Your daughter is one sharp gal, Betty! A prenuptial agreement. That's exactly what this is."

They walked off hand-in-hand, pleased with themselves. They got married a few days later. But it wasn't long before Mom showed up and asked for the papers back. No one was surprised, and no one missed Johnny.

We were gathering for a summer barbeque in our Covina home. Aunt Evelyn sat at my dining room table playing Gin Rummy with Grandma Davis. I was dusting and getting ready for everyone to arrive. Mom had told us she was coming with her new boyfriend, Paul. "I would be embarrassed if I were Betty, going from man to man to man," Aunt Evelyn said.

Grandma Davis chuckled. "My younger daughter never had any sense when it came to men." Immediately uncomfortable, she shot a glance at me, adding, "But she chose well when she married Al, of course."

Evelyn nodded. "That goes without saying, Mom. Al is a good man. But let's face it. Betty flaunts herself, nearly throws herself at any man that walks in the door."

Grandma Davis said, "She's never had any trouble attracting men, that's for sure. She's always been pretty and charismatic."

"Hmph, that's not what I mean, Mom," Evelyn said. "I guess she is pretty in a particular sort of way." She touched her hair, bringing attention to herself. "But it's more than that. Surely, you've seen it over the years. Betty is, well, rather cheap, don't you think?"

The backdoor opened, and Mom's shrill voice echoed through the house. "We're here!" She walked into the room on the arm of her newest companion. "I'd like to introduce you to Paul." The handsome man with dark hair smiled widely. "He's an air traffic controller." My mother seemed proud of him.

"Hello, ladies, I'm happy to meet you," Paul said. He smiled at Mom and then at us.

Mom introduced us around the room, and Paul politely nodded in recognition. When Mom was happy, she filled the room with her expansive joy as she did now. She and Paul were obviously caught up in a romance that made them both seem younger and more vibrant. I couldn't help but be hopeful about this one.

I glanced over at Aunt Evelyn's face and was startled to see her eyes fierce and angry. *She's jealous!*

Dan and Bill walked in. "Hello. You must be Paul," Dan said as he shook Paul's hand. "This is Bill." Bill and Paul shook hands. "Paul, do you want to come outside with Bill and me to get the barbecue going?" Paul agreed, and the men went out to the backyard. I could always count on Dan being charming when it was time to play host to a party.

Smiling, Mom plopped down next to Grandma Davis at the table. "Mom, what do you think of Paul? He's handsome, isn't he?"

Grandma Davis had a smile on her face and was about to agree when Aunt Evelyn interjected. "Where do you find all of these men, Betty? One after another after another."

Mom's face fell. "I don't—"

"I mean, there was Ed and that other guy who was so skinny."

"That was Mark," Mom murmured.

And you even married Johnny, right? How long did that last?"

Grandma Davis looked at Evelyn and back at Mom. And then she joined my aunt in taunting my mother. "Well, Betty, you have to admit, you have gone through quite a few men in your time."

"Stop it. Why can't you be happy for me?' Mom pleaded with them.

"Betty, how many men? Add them up. What's the total?" Evelyn's cutting words caused Grandma and I to gasp audibly. Mom's eyes filled with tears, and she fidgeted with the sleeve of her sweater, unable to look up at her sneering sister and chastising mother. It hurt me to see her toyed with by the two most powerful women in her life. I didn't know what to say or do. Mom had always been the one who hurt people. I'd never seen her put to such a disadvantage.

Mom tried to withstand this exposing onslaught of truth. Unable to find words, she finally cradled her face in her hands and cried. Humiliated. Unprotected. Crushed. Unable to calm down, she stood up and scurried to the bathroom. I heard her sob for a few minutes. I stared at my aunt and grandma as they kept up their commentary on Mom's dating life.

After a couple of minutes, I knocked faintly on the bathroom door. "Mom?"

"I'm—I'm fine, Pat," she said through the door, still weeping.

Aunt Evelyn looked up at me with a smug look on her face. "Pat, you, of all people, should know what damage your mother has done to others." She stood up and stormed out, heading to the backyard.

Grandma wouldn't make eye contact with me. I knew she was ashamed, as she should have been. But I helped her up, and we joined the men by the barbeque. Mom showed up, eyes red but with new lipstick on her warm smile. She cuddled up to Paul as if nothing had happened.

Missing Puzzle Piece

For years, Dan had been unhappy in his job. I encouraged him to start his own business, and in 1973, we started a mold-making business. We sold nearly everything we had, and I pinched every penny to get us through. Dan was a master mold-maker, and he serviced every order we had.

Meanwhile, Mom, Aunt Evelyn, and I continued to take turns caring for Grandma Davis. On one particular afternoon, it was Aunt Evelyn's turn to pick up Grandma. Aunt Evelyn arrived a bit early, and she and I sat in the backyard, sharing a pot of tea, waiting for my mother and grandma to arrive for the handoff.

I was unhappy in my marriage, constantly rehearsing where things went wrong inside my mind. *Dan was so angry when I miscarried. Eric was our gift. Our one child my body could take to term.* I was so preoccupied with my misery that I could hardly focus on Aunt Evelyn. But I hoped to get her talking about herself to pass the time until Grandma arrived.

"Tell me, Aunt Evelyn, how was it to have Janny and Roy home over Memorial Day weekend?" She answered, and I nodded, but my mind shifted to Mom and Dad. I flashed on my miscarriages.

It must have been awful for Mom to deal with so many losses. I knew how that felt. Losing our first two pregnancies strained my marriage. I lifted the pot and poured more hot tea into our mugs. Breathing in the aromatic freshness of the Earl Grey, I passed Evelyn her mug.

Aunt Evelyn was recounting details of the barbecue she and Bill had hosted. Without checking myself, I interrupted. "It must have been hard on Mom to go through so much loss when I was little. All of those miscarriages."

Plopping her mug on the glass table, Aunt Evelyn looked at me with confusion written all over her face. "What? What are you talking about, Pat?"

Clearly lost in my murky thoughts, I mumbled, "Uh, I was curious about Mom's miscarriages."

"Your mother *never* had a miscarriage."

I was confused. "I remember my mom being in bed and massive amounts of blood on the sheets. I know Grandma tried to hide it from me, but I saw all of it. And I remember the distinct smell of blood. It happened a lot." I was surprised I shared that, but I was eager to have a truthful picture of my parents' relationship.

Aunt Evelyn frowned. Pausing, she looked off momentarily as though she was seeking guidance from the trees. She took a sip from her cup, straightened in her chair, and spoke. "Pat, you're a grown woman now with your own child."

"Yes, and what are you getting at?" I searched her face, wondering what she was revealing. *Speak, Evelyn.*

"I think you deserve to know the truth, Pat." She leaned in and cleared her throat.

I sat forward in my chair, braced for her disclosure.

"But don't tell your mom that I told you this."

"Told me what?"

"Pat," she whispered, "your mother didn't have miscarriages. She had abortions."

I felt my stomach turn. "Abortions? Wait, what?"

Light-headed and perplexed, I looked at my aunt, waiting for this to make sense. Without breaking from my gaze, she sat back against the cushion. Finally, she grabbed her mug, sipped her tea, and studied the roses.

"I…I…don't understand." I tried again to say something. "Wait, why?" I thought I was going to vomit. "Were they even legal back then?"

"No, they weren't, Pat. That's why it was all so upsetting to us. We never knew if she'd survive them, but Betty insisted."

Abortions. That thought had never even crossed my mind.

"Wait. What are you telling me?"

I stared across the table, viewing my memories, not Evelyn's smug face.

"How many abortions did she have?"

"Five, Pat. She had five of them." Her disapproving tone was clearly understood as she refilled our cups.

I could barely take this in. *Allie and I could have had five siblings. And here I was, feeling sorry for Mom. She aborted her babies! My father's babies! My brothers and sisters!*

"What about Dad? Wasn't he upset?"

Aunt Evelyn scoffed. "Your father was devastated. But your mother did *not* want any more children." She stopped herself. "I'm sorry, Pat. I didn't mean it that way." My aunt had a way of saying something awful and pretending it was a mistake. "But let's be honest here, just between us. We know she's never been a good mother, not to you or Allie. It isn't in her nature to care for anyone but herself."

"Aunt Evelyn!" I stood up quickly. I hated hearing her say something so awful about *my* mom.

"Someone has to tell you the truth, Pat. Everyone in this family keeps so many secrets to protect your mother. Well, I'm tired of making everything about her."

I sat down again, stunned into silence. I hadn't realized how much resentment Aunt Evelyn had toward Mom. Sure, I resented my mom. But it was different. She was my mother. It made my skin crawl to hear Aunt Evelyn spout venom against her own sister.

She kept going. "But we knew that Al couldn't keep her tied down. You know, she never loved your father."

I stood up and grabbed the teapot. "I think we've run out of hot water. I'll go get some more." I stomped into the kitchen. I held onto the sink to steady myself as my emotions swirled. *My mother had abortions, not miscarriages.* The compassion I'd been feeling for her vanished, replaced by loathing. Yet the hatred that my aunt expressed for Mom offended me at the same time.

> *Someone has to tell you the truth, Pat. Everyone in this family keeps so many secrets to protect your mother.*

I thought I might be sick again, but Mom opened the front door before I could move to the bathroom so Grandma Davis could enter with her walker. "Hello! We're here."

Aunt Evelyn suddenly appeared at my side and grabbed my forearm tightly. "Remember, you promised that you wouldn't tell your mom I told you."

I wasn't ready to promise anything at that particular moment. Forcing a smile at Mom, I excused myself to go and check on Eric, the best part of my life. He was sleeping soundly on his bed, exhausted from playing at the park with his friends earlier. I studied his face, awed by his rosy cheeks and long, thick eyelashes. I loved him more than life itself. After two miscarriages, it was hard for me to understand Mom's choices.

Because I Knew You Were Mine

After that heartbreaking revelation from Aunt Evelyn, I had trouble finding my footing. My marriage to Dan had become more difficult as Dan and Eric began butting heads. At eleven, Eric was tall for his age, had a thick head of hair like his father, and an intelligent, mischievous twinkle in his eye. Full of energy and curiosity, just like me, he was always asking questions about everything imaginable. Like most older boys entering their teens, Eric was all the more animated and less likely to obey us. Dan's short fuse regarding Eric became an even larger source of conflict between us. I felt that Eric needed his Grandpa Al more than ever.

Then Dad told me he and Alice were moving away from California to southern Oregon with their little white poodle. They hoped the green beauty of Gold Hill would be the idyllic setting for their later years. I didn't know how to tell him that his grandson needed him or that I needed him to talk to me about what Evelyn had told me. Instead, I kept silent. When the only parent I had relied on drove off to Oregon, I went into an emotional tailspin.

The implications of the abortions—not one but five—kept swirling through my head. *What role did Dad play? Why did he allow it to happen? Did he know beforehand, or did Mom get the abortions as soon as she realized she was pregnant? Granted, birth control wasn't readily available in the 1940s, other than diaphragms and condoms, but few knew about them. Still, couldn't something have been done to prevent those pregnancies?* The turmoil inside me continued to grow until I talked Dan into taking us on a road trip to visit Dad and Alice when Eric's school year ended.

To take the trip, we needed to get a newer car. Dan and I couldn't agree on things. He wanted a particular green '71 Buick Skylark with a gold Landau roof. But I had a premonition about that car falling apart as we drove down the street. The next morning, I told Dan about my premonition and warned him. "Don't buy that green car!"

Dan did not listen. "No, no, no, Pat, let's buy it. The dealership sells it with a warranty. They'll fix any problems for up to a year!" He came home that night, driving the green Skylark.

The trip to Oregon was a few weeks off, so we had the chance to see if my dream would come true. Dan left early and drove our new car to work. I was sipping my coffee and reading the paper when, to my surprise, he soon walked back to the house. He found me in the kitchen and handed me this metal thing.

"What's that?" Before he could answer, I realized he was holding the entire lock assembly from the car door, with Dan's keyring dangling.

He confessed. "It came out with the key."

"What do you mean?"

"I unlocked the car, and this whole thing lifted out as I tried to remove my key!" We burst into laughter at the oddity of such a thing. Then I reminded him, "Do you recall my dream about that car?"

Dan didn't find that amusing.

The key lock was simply a portend of things to come. I was a regular visitor to Reynold's Buick, with one thing or another needing repair. There was a place where the chrome wasn't right on the bumper. When they fixed it, the bumper was placed on the car crooked. Then, the vehicle leaked when I drove it through the carwash. It was ridiculous and irritating but also funny. "You should listen, Dan, when I have a dream." Dan insisted that it was a great buy and dug in his heels.

Eric's school finally let out for the summer, and we packed up for our trip north. Dan humored me with my desire to see Dad. Mainly, he was obsessed with fishing in the Rogue River, which was right across the road from their home. Our new green Skylark was packed to the gills for the road trip. Eric was good-natured about the long car ride, knowing Oregon would offer a lot of new exploring adventures when we got there.

That stretch of the I-5 was six hundred miles of straight road up Central California and lovely with its sunny weather. The road became windy once we passed Mount Shasta, and our elevation rose. Soon, there were sprinkles and then rain. Dan's cursing woke Eric and me up from resting our eyes.

Drip. Drip. Drip.

The windshield leak had returned, and there was a steady plopping of water onto Dan's left leg. It continued for five hours despite his attempt to block it with his handkerchief. By now, his leg was saturated, and the water drained in a mini stream down his lower leg into his shoe.

Eric and I had to practice super self-control and not laugh. I certainly didn't want to set Dan off. Instead, while exchanging knowing looks, we gathered newspapers and clothing that could be pushed below the windshield to catch the rainwater flow. Once a piece was saturated and dripping, we replaced it with more material until the rain finally let up.

We soon forgot about the car problems once we arrived in the Grant's Pass area. We were all mesmerized by the lush beauty, the roar of the river, and the serenity of the country. Dad and Alice welcomed us, and Dan and my father did their best to avoid each other.

We fell into an easy routine during the week we were there. Alice puttered around the kitchen and then went about her normal pattern. I enjoyed my coffee and newspaper time in the morning with Dad. My father would take a nap in the afternoon. Otherwise, we sat reading together in the backyard or watching television. The conversation was pleasant but superficial for the most part. I had a question to ask him but couldn't quite get up the nerve to broach the subject.

Eric was on a continuous mission to explore the countryside. I don't know if Dan was interested in joining his son or if it seemed the best way to avoid sitting down and talking with my father. But my son and husband would take the car on adventures each day. They even went fishing together, crossing the street to the incredible Rogue River. Dan was clearly outside his comfort zone. But this father-son duo was successful, and we enjoyed some delicious fish dinners.

I could see the tension wearing on Dan. I didn't want something to aggravate him in front of Dad, so I suggested we leave a day early, and I got no objections. So, I packed, and we loaded the car with our suitcases to go the following day.

Dan and Eric left to fill the car with gas and get food for our trip back. I knew this was my last chance to talk to Dad privately. Alice made herself scarce, and I courageously took the opportunity to speak with him. He seemed to want the same thing. To my surprise, he was the one who took the lead.

"How are you doing?" Dad asked. "I mean, I don't want to pry."

"No, I want to talk to you, Dad." Immediately, I had to fight back the tears.

"It's Dan, isn't it, Pat?" My father's tone was serious, expecting the worst of my husband.

I nodded. "The marriage is in trouble. I thought having Eric would help, but it has only made things harder." He seemed to understand that statement. "But I think I've come up with an idea that could help. We're thinking about setting up a tool-making business together. He'll do the tool-making, and I'll take care of the books."

He frowned. "I don't want to be negative, Pat, but…" he stopped and took a deep breath. "You know how I feel about Dan."

A deep emotional pain washed over me, remembering how Dad had refused to attend my wedding. "Yes."

Dad's jaw clenched. He wasn't the kind who said, "I told you so." Instead, he said, "Pat, I'm sorry." I could tell he was figuring out how to put something into words. "I don't want to discourage you about this company. But I don't think Dan has the nerves necessary to run a business well. But you do, Pat. You're perfect for running a business. So if you want to start a company, I think you should do it on your own. Keep Dan out of it."

His honesty about Dan threw me, and I was pleasantly surprised by the confidence he had in me. I stammered, "What kind of business could I start by myself? On my own as a woman? I have Eric and the house; I can't do that alone. Besides…"

"Dan wouldn't let you."

He knew what I was going to say! I sat back in my chair. I had expected Dad to support me in this plan. He didn't know that we'd already started the business and had sold nearly everything we had to invest in it. A bolt of panic shot through me. *Have I made another huge mistake?*

"Dad, I just hate being stuck at home all the time, and he doesn't want me working. He says it's because I should be home to take care of Eric when he comes home from school. I am! I leave work in time to meet him after school. I get him to team practices and keep stats at all his games. I'm not neglecting him or running from being a mom. But I want to work too."

My dad nodded. "I know you are great at doing books and keeping order. But Dan does see things from a traditional point of view." I thought that was a nice way to put it.

"The only way I can do something with my life is to do it with Dan. That's just how it is."

A sadness swept over his face. "I understand, Patsy." We both knew my options were limited as long as I stayed married to Dan.

I was anxious to change the topic to why I wanted this visit.

Refilling our mugs and emptying his ashtray, I returned to the dark walnut dining table and sat in the chair right across from him.

"Dad, I have to talk to you about something."

"Hmm, okay, what is it?" He lit another cigarette and played with his lighter.

"Well, I remember when I was a little girl, Mom was always in bed. She was sick or something. Depressed maybe? Sometimes, I saw blood on the sheets, and there was always that awful metallic smell."

He nodded. I couldn't read him. His face was utterly blank. It made me nervous to continue. I took a deep breath and let it out slowly.

"Someone told me that Mom had abortions when I was young."

"Who told you?" He dropped the lighter, and smoke billowed from his face. "Your Aunt Evelyn?"

"Does it matter, Dad?"

"I guess not. It makes sense to me that she'd try to drive a wedge between you and your mother."

"Well, is it true?"

He teetered back in his chair with a pained look, staring off as if traveling back in time. I waited. Finally, the chair slammed back to the floor, and he said, "Yes, it's true.

I had believed it, but hearing Dad acknowledge it seared my heart. I couldn't understand how my father could do this; why he wouldn't have tried to stop her. They were his children as much as hers. "I don't understand, Dad. You both decided to abort your babies?"

A deep anger flashed in his eyes as he inhaled his cigarette. "Oh, no, those babies weren't mine, Pat."

I was unable to speak. My mind couldn't comprehend what Dad said. "They weren't yours?" I let that sink in. *Mom had been with other men while married to my father.* "Are you saying that mom was having affairs?"

His eyes answered before his mouth did. "I wanted to protect you from all of this, Patsy."

I just stared at him. *My mother was sleeping with other men and aborted five of my siblings.* Everyone had known. Grandpa Roy and Grandma Davis. Aunt Evelyn. And worst of all, Dad had known.

"But—"

He raised his hand to stop me. "It was what she wanted, Pat. That's just who Betty was and is."

Then it hit me—somehow, Allie and I had been carried to term. *Why?*

"But what about me, Dad? Why wasn't I aborted."

He answered quickly. "Because I wouldn't give your mother fifty dollars for the abortion."

I was shaking, realizing she never really wanted to be my mother. "Why not, Dad?"

My dad looked straight at me and tenderly said, "Because I knew *you* were *mine*."

I stared at him, speechless. Mercifully, Eric ran into the kitchen and shouted, "Dad says we gotta get on the road!" I was never so relieved in my life.

I got to my feet. "Yes, I guess it's time to leave." Alice reappeared, and we hugged goodbye. I climbed into the car as quickly as possible. As Dan pulled the car out of the driveway, he gave me a curious glance but said nothing.

There was nothing I wanted to explain. "Let's wave goodbye, Eric!" I called out with my hand extended out the window. Eric leaned out of the car window, "Bye, Grandpa Al! Bye, Grandma Alice!"

> *My dad looked straight at me and tenderly said, "Because I knew you were mine."*

I rolled the window up and turned on the radio. I had no interest in talking. Questions filled my mind. *How could my mother not only abandon me and Allie but also be unfaithful to Dad? There were numerous pregnancies, and how did Mom have the gall to ask my dad to support her abortions financially? Was paying for the procedures his way of coping with her betrayal? Had he considered raising the children from her affairs as his own? And how could Dad still take her back time and again? How had he forgiven her, if that is even possible?*

The lush Oregon views sped past my window, but I didn't see the beauty. All I could see was confusion and betrayal. I felt a deep disgust for my mother. But now I was torn inside. My dad, the man I relied on and trusted, had become someone I no longer recognized.

We'd driven for hours, the radio filling the silence as the darkness of night erased the beauty we had enjoyed. "Dan, we need to stop for gas soon. We are getting very close to E."

"I see that, Pat. If I recall, we have at least twenty-five miles until the next town."

"Dan! We won't make it." We bantered back and forth, both a little panicked.

From the backseat, Eric said, "There's a gas station coming up. You know, the one with the orange ball?"

Dan snapped at him. "Stop lying!"

Eric said, "Mom! I'm not making it up. I can see it!"

I wanted to give Eric the benefit of the doubt. I pointed to the speedometer. "Let's see how far it is."

Dan and I stared into the black horizon, not seeing any hope of a gas station.

Minutes passed. "Look, Mom! Now, do you see it?" I looked out again, and sure enough, there was the glow in the distance of an orange 76 Union gas sign. It had been three miles away.

"Looks like we can make it there just fine. Isn't Eric an incredible kid?" I was shocked he could see that far.

Dan's silence spoke volumes.

A Choice, a Response

"Alan just died, Patsy. I can't believe it." Startled and awakened by the early morning phone call in November 1973, I recognized my dear cousin's voice immediately. Marilyn and I didn't talk regularly, but we caught up over the phone about twice a year. "Marilyn! What are you saying?" I carried the phone into the bathroom and shut the door so Dan wouldn't wake up.

"His department was fighting a fire, Patsy." Marilyn, my dear cousin in Ohio, was sobbing on the other end. "He surveyed the crew as they went into the house. The smoke was horrible. The house collapsed, Patsy! Alan was rushed to the hospital with smoke inhalation." She could barely get the words out through her sobs. "His captain called and said, 'There's no rush, but to come to the hospital when you can.' But, Patsy, when I got there," Marilyn paused, breathing loudly and sniffling with each breath. "I found out he had already died!"

I shivered in shock as the chill of her news matched the brisk air of the morning. She and Alan were newlyweds—just married for two years and discussing having their first child. Tears were welling in my eyes. How could this be happening?

"Marilyn! I'm so sorry. Do you want me to come out?" I heard her inhale deeply, probably relieved she had gotten the awful news out.

Marilyn, a practical schoolteacher, replied, "No, not now. It's cold and miserable here. As much as I want you here, I can't manage a visit right now. My mom is on her way, though."

I felt somewhat rebuffed. I knew she was a mess, but how could I help if I didn't go to her? Why was she pushing me away? Aunt Gertrude would be helpful, but would she offer the kind of support I sensed Marilyn was asking for?

She interrupted my thoughts. "But Patsy, will you visit in a few months? I will need you to help me with the house by then. There will be so much to…" Her voice broke. She didn't need to finish her thought. We both knew what she was thinking. Once the school year was over, it would be time to sort through her husband's things, clean out the basement and garage, and adjust to his forever absence.

I was glad I could be of help. And it was good to know someone wanted me. "Of course, Marilyn. I'll come to help." She was the closest thing to a sister I had ever had. We planned that I would fly to Ohio in the spring. I would be honored to be there for my cousin, Marilyn.

> *"Of course, Marilyn. I'll come to help." She was the closest thing to a sister I had ever had.*

Dan was livid when I told him about my spring plans over morning coffee and eggs. "You made this decision without talking to me first?"

"She needs me, Dan. Her husband died! What could I say? She's family."

"You could say, 'No, I have a husband to take care of.' I'm your family, Pat!"

"You're a grown man, Dan. Certainly, you can take care of yourself and Eric for one week while I'm in Ohio."

That upset him further. "You mean you're not taking Eric with you?"

"No, he's a twelve-year-old boy. What would he do in Ohio while we're packing up the house? Dan, be reasonable." When those words came out of my mouth, I almost laughed. When was Dan ever reasonable?

He stomped out of the room and slammed the door behind him. For a moment, I faltered, thinking I would call Marilyn back and tell her I couldn't come. But when I imagined telling her that I wouldn't help her deal with her husband's death because *my* husband was too childish to take care of himself and his son for seven days, I just couldn't make the call. I was going, no matter what Dan said.

In the spring of 1974, I boarded a plane to visit my cousin for one week. Ohio was burgeoning with all a Midwest spring offers. It was restoring for me to be there, even as Marilyn and I faced a somber, sad task.

Dan called me every day, relentlessly demanding. "Pat, you need to come home right now!" He seemed desperate, like a small boy wanting his mommy. I didn't leave Ohio. I stayed the week and helped Marilyn all I could. It was a precious time together, and I was glad to be there. She needed my emotional support and help with the chore of packing and moving. We both needed the time to reminisce and feel the familiarity of our kinship.

When I returned home a week later, Dan refused to pick me up at the airport. I took a taxi and arrived home to find Eric in the house by himself. He was watching television and drinking chocolate milk. The house felt so different. It was a mess and felt like a house of grief—just like Marilyn's.

"Where's Dad?" I leaned over and tussled his hair, glad to see my boy.

Eric shrugged. "I don't know. He packed up his clothes and left this morning."

"He's gone? Moved out?"

Eric nodded. "Yep."

"And he left you here all by yourself?"

Eric finally looked up at me. "Yep, I've been here alone all day." He seemed resigned to the situation. *Like mother, like son.*

In my mind's eye, I could see my twelve-year-old self running upstairs, shocked to see my mom's empty closet. My heart broke for Eric, knowing what it felt like for a parent to leave without explanation. I hugged Eric and promised I would find him.

After fixing Eric something to eat, I drove over to our shop. Sure enough, Dan's car was parked out front. I found him in the office, smoking at his desk, a couple of suitcases parked up against the wall. His gaze was distant, and I was incredulous. His olive complexion was grey; he looked unusually thin. In just a week, he'd dropped twenty pounds! What happened to my husband?

I stood with my hands on my hips. "Do you want to tell me what's going on?"

His dulled eyes slowly turned to look into mine. Then, like a flick of a switch, he unleashed a rage that scared me. He stood up, eyes flashing and teeth bared, and bellowed, "You left me. Now I'm leaving you!"

"I went to visit my family for a week." I smacked my hand on the doorframe. "Seven days, only seven days." I tried to calm down. In a softer tone, I reminded him, "I didn't leave you, Dan."

He shifted back to a shadowy figure and shook his head as he sat back down. Dan was a tall man—a big man. But he looked small and weak at that moment, like a lost little boy. He was disheveled and unshaven, and he had obviously slept in his clothes.

The change in his appearance was astonishing. My heart softened. Trying to respond in a way that didn't further distress him, I picked up one of the suitcases. "I'm back now. Are you coming home, Dan?" I walked to the door and waited.

He snuffed out his cigarette, stood up, and picked up the other suitcase. He never answered but followed me outside and got into his car. I got into mine, and I followed him back home. Whatever little trust Dan and I shared was crushed.

I honestly don't know when Dan started his many affairs, perhaps early in our marriage, but I knew he wasn't always where he said he was. He was quite capable of lying to me, and I'll admit, I didn't want to face the fact that he was going out on me.

Any pretense that our marriage was intact shattered one afternoon later that year when I puttered around the kitchen and straightened up the counters. We kept matchbooks in a drawer, and a few had fallen out of their organizer. One caught my eye—it was open and had handwriting inside. "Meet you at 3:30, M." The hot pain flared in my chest as I attempted to breathe. I could no longer deny that Dan was having another affair.

I insisted that we go to counseling, and to my amazement, he reluctantly agreed. My doctor referred us to a therapist named Jim Parker, or Dr. Jim as we called him. Oddly, the night before our first session, I had a premonition of meeting a man in a light brown leisure suit. I wondered what that was about and if it had anything to do with what was going on between Dan and me. But I went into the session with naïve hope.

Dan and I sat in separate chairs across from Dr. Jim's desk. He was a middle-aged man wearing a light brown leisure suit. I was not surprised.

"We need help with our marriage," Dan said.

Rather than responding to Dan, Dr. Jim looked at me and scolded me. "You can expect a man to stray if you withhold sex from your husband."

I was taken completely aback by his assumption. That was not our problem. The few times I'd declined Dan's advances, I was sick, and Dan was quite understanding. My surprise quickly turned to anger, but I felt I could not express that emotion there. All I could say was, "I don't do that."

Dr. Jim looked confused. Apparently, the good doctor presumed that the responsibility for a man's infidelity was laid at the feet of a sexually withholding wife. He glanced at Dan, who shrugged his shoulders and nodded in agreement with me. "We have no trouble in the bedroom."

"It's only been five times! And it was because I was sick."

"It's true," Dan confirmed.

That seemed to strip Dr. Jim of his sole marriage problem solution, and there wasn't much more he had to offer. He squirmed for lack of anything else to say.

But Dan, a leader in manipulation skills, threw the therapist a lifeline of some good ol' boy banter, which Dr. Jim gratefully grabbed onto. Soon, the two men bonded around the idea that, even if I was great in bed, the problem with Dan's behavior was due to something I was doing wrong or failing to do at all.

I should have stopped therapy with Dr. Jim at this point.

Dan quickly fooled Dr. Jim into agreeing that there was no purpose to his coming to future sessions since the problem was mine, not ours—and most certainly not Dan's. I had neither the insight nor the willpower to contradict the joint opinion of these two men. I should have left these sessions. But before I knew what was happening, Dan bowed out of the process, and I continued to meet with Dr. Jim every week for two years.

She Should Have Been Locked Up

Mom flitted in and out with Grandma Davis for just over two years. They both fawned over my teenager, Eric, as much as he'd tolerate. My brother Allie had married, had two boys, and practiced medicine a few hours north of Covina. As family life allowed, we'd all gather with Dan's family and mine for holidays, kids' sports events, and birthdays.

Mom and I never talked about her secret life of other men and abortions. I was too ashamed to tell anyone what my parents had done, so I stuffed down my feelings and carried on. Mom and I often met for breakfast. To my surprise, she was consistently learning new things, was helpful, and was sometimes observant. Mom was an avid reader and, in her way, looked for guidance in various churches and other spiritual practices. From time to time, she had surprising insights into her behavior. Still, for the most part, she tried my patience with her impulsiveness and ditziness. The bond between us was simple—we both liked to play cards.

I found new evidence of Dan's numerous affairs, and yet we continued our marriage as if nothing was amiss; we lived together, argued together, had sex together, co-parented our son, and worked together. I thought about my father, who didn't stand up for himself when my mom betrayed him. Like father, like daughter. Everyone knew what Dan was up to, but I held my head high, pretending everything was fine.

All the while, I went once a week to see Dr. Jim as if on autopilot. I arrived in a state of rage and deep despair, handed him sixty dollars, and told him he wasn't helping me. Dr. Jim had trained in a type of psychology that focuses heavily on dream interpretation. He took the money and asked me to tell him about my dreams that week. In actuality, I was so overwhelmed that the only thing I could talk about were the glimpses of my unconscious.

I thought about my father, who didn't stand up for himself when my mom had betrayed him. Like father, like daughter.

I did what he said. We analyzed hundreds of dreams, all indicating that I felt trapped and angry in a horrible marriage. I returned each week feeling as powerless and miserable as the day I first entered his office—insight but no action.

This went on for two years. Two years.

But a true miracle happened. In 1979, My mother reached *her* limit of watching me tolerate my marriage and my therapy. Mom might not have understood how to relate to infants and children (and to be clear, she did not), but she could boast expertise in troubled relationships with men. Perhaps Mom and I could have bonded over other shared interests, but as it turned out, when my marriage was disintegrating and I was sinking deeper into a dark place, Mom saw precisely what was happening, and she "got" it.

"Patsy!" Frustrated, Mom confronted me one afternoon. "You've been going to that guy forever, and you're not getting any better."

I sighed and agreed.

"So, I'm going with you to the next session."

"You're what?"

"Yes, I'm going with you, and we're going to get you moving along here." And with that declaration, the decision was made.

Dr. Jim was slightly startled to see Mom and me at the door, but he let us both in without protest. We sat down, and Mom took the lead.

"Doctor, my daughter isn't getting any better, so I'm here today to get this ball rolling." She stared at him.

Dr. Jim sat there, not sure what to say. "Do you have something you'd like to say?" he stammered.

"No. You're the therapist. Do your job."

Dr. Jim seemed perplexed as to what his job might entail.

"Go ahead," my mother urged him. "Ask my daughter some questions."

That was the guidance he needed. Turning to me, he asked me about my most recent dream.

I sputtered in a burst of anger. "What? My mother is in the room with us, and you ask me to tell you a dream?"

Dr. Jim dismissed me and looked over at my mother, repeating what he had said to Dan in therapy years before. "Isn't she beautiful when she's mad?"

Mom frowned. "Do you know that she drinks in the morning?"

Dr. Jim looked bewildered. He knew so little about what I was doing with my pain.

Mom continued. "She plays Solitaire all day and then drinks herself silly. You know, Doctor, people drink because of physical or emotional pain or because of something we do not want to face or are afraid to face."

Dr. Jim stared at her as if she was speaking a different language.

"Doctor, Pat and Dan have been talking and talking and talking. Don't you think my daughter should take some action?"

"Oh, yes, I don't intend to let her go on for another year like this."

My mother scoffed, and I clenched my fists. We three sat there in silence for a few moments. Reaching down, my mother grabbed her purse, and I thought she might be preparing to leave. Instead, she pulled out a sheet of folded stationery. She handed it to me and commanded, "Here, Pat. Read this out loud. I want the doctor here to hear this."

Gulping, I took the page and started reading.

"It's a letter my mom wrote me," I began.

> Dear Patsy,
>
> Dan was not working, so you got him an apprentice job where you worked. You worked to save enough money for a down payment on a house. Dan wanted you to have a baby because it would make him less likely to be drafted for the Korean War. So, you stayed home. You had a baby. You sold Avon and helped him get started on his own business.
>
> He bought a boat.
>
> He bought a bigger shop.
>
> He bought a Lincoln.
>
> He bought a bigger boat and a truck.
>
> You have helped him all along. So why do you feel guilty if you want to separate to find yourself? Dan has too powerful of a personality for you to rebuff. I am concerned about you because I care very much about you. I am right behind you all the way. You can come here anytime.
>
> Love, Mom

I looked at Dr. Jim, feeling exposed, not knowing what to do next. Regaining some semblance of composure, and I suspect trying to at least sound like a therapist, Dr. Jim turned to me and asked, "Pat, is there something you'd like to say to your mother?"

That stopped me short. No one had ever asked me that question before. At that moment, I realized that I had a lot I wanted to say to her. And I decided to unload years of things I'd carried on my shoulders but wanted to communicate directly to her.

Like a reporter, I looked at my mom and began to speak out about those things she had done that had hurt me. "The shock of learning about your abortions and about other men you slept with besides Dad has haunted me." Realizing she was in direct line of my fire, Mom gasped and began frantically searching between my face and Dr. Jim's, needing reassurance and safety. I gave her none.

"You have no idea how my heart ached as a kid. I was left with Aunt Gertrude while Dad was at war. She was an angel who cared for me and you; you were somewhere." Suddenly aware of what I was doing, my heart pounded, my face flushed, and my throat felt like it was closing. "When we were forced to be a family when Dad came home, you didn't pay attention to me. You stayed in bed all the time."

Mom looked to Dr. Jim, "I did. I—"

He motioned her to be silent and nodded for me to continue. "Mom! You didn't even feed me. I still keep crackers and water by my bed in case I get hungry in the night." Mom stared at me blankly.

"Do you remember? I had warts all over and was anemic because I was malnourished." I was weeping as I spoke. Dr. Jim was riveted and marveled at my sharing. Mom's eyes were like saucers.

I focused then on Dr. Jim's kind gaze while recounting my wounds. "The worst day of my life was when I came home from school, and you were gone. Pork chops on the stove." I let out a sob from deep inside. "You took Allie away! Do you know what it was like, running around the house frantically looking for you? Your closet was empty. So was Allie's. Mom! I was all alone. I can still feel the panic. All afternoon, by myself, I waited for Dad to come home. I-I was devastated!"

I took a breath as tears flowed down my face. So much raw emotion had surfaced. I glanced up at my mother and saw that she was crying quietly. And to my utter surprise, so was Dr. Jim.

My mother reached out for my hand, but I pulled it away. "Patsy, I know I hurt you. I have no excuse except that I didn't know what else to do."

I never heard Mom speak like this. Glad to stop my rant, I watched her keenly as she shared.

"I lived in an emotional black hole, sleeping most of the time, desperately unhappy, and lost and afraid."

"Afraid of *what*, Mother?" I was incensed.

"Afraid of everything, Patsy! Everything!" She paused to blow her nose and tried to regain her composure. "Your dad did his best, but Al didn't understand me. He still doesn't and never will. Being with him is torture to me." Mom now wept openly.

"So you slept with other men?" She covered her face with her hands, but even though I saw her break down in front of me, I couldn't stop myself. A lifetime of pain spewed from my heart. "And what about the abortions?" I realized my voice was shrill. Dr. Jim put his hand on my mom's arm. That move allowed me to take a deep breath.

Mom uncovered her face and wiped the wetness with a couple of tissues. In a small voice, almost too quiet to hear, she said, "I have no excuse. Each time I got pregnant, I would look at you and say to myself, 'Look what an awful mother you are to her.' I just couldn't do that to another child. I thought about suicide every time. But I guess I was even too afraid to go through with that."

She collapsed back into the chair, defeated, and stripped emotionally bare. She'd never revealed anything so vulnerable to me before. I saw her not as my mother but as a stranger. Someone I'd not met before. Someone broken, perhaps beyond repair. I almost felt sorry for her, although that was further than I was ready to go then.

"But you never *really* thought about me, Mom," I whispered. "You left me."

"I thought about you a lot, Pat. I didn't know what to do about you—*with* you. I didn't know how to take care of you. Or Allie, either, once he was born. That's why Al got custody of both of you."

That angered me. "You lost custody of Allie because you didn't take care of him. He nearly froze to death because you were out drinking or picking up men."

Shame settled on her face. She had no counter. She wiped her eyes and said emphatically, "You want me to say it? Okay, I will. I was a horrible wife to your dad and a horrible mom to you and Allie. I should have been *locked up*, Patsy. Locked up and never released. Never."

Nothing had prepared me for that moment. I'd never imagined my mother had much awareness that I even existed, let alone find out that she realized, to some extent, that her actions had hurt me so profoundly. She shape-shifted again, this time from a stranger to another human being who was more than simply my mother. I saw her in the context of her entire existence: as a woman who was desperate to be loved, the daughter of parents who undermined her self-confidence at every turn, a human being who suffered from mental illness without help, and as someone who suffered the pain of knowing she had hurt other people. Empathy? Was that even possible?

"Mom," I reached out and touched her hand. She looked up at me with sad eyes.

Dr. Jim stood up and said, "The session has gone over time, but I didn't want to stop you." He gestured for us to share a hug. The hug was brief, but I felt so close to her. Still angry, but she was there for me.

Out of his office, we quietly walked to the parking lot. "Patsy, you know I love you, don't you?"

The trance of being seen and loved broken, I returned to caretaking her. "I know, Mom, I know you do."

I watched her pull away from her parking spot. Driving home in a daze, I tried to sort out what had just happened and what it meant. I looked at people I passed on the street. At the red lights, I glanced over at the drivers in the other cars. For them, it was just another day. But for me, the world had shifted on its axis.

Mother-Daughter Bond?

Until that therapy session, I'd never seen this self-aware side of my mother. I could see now that she loved me and was on a quest to heal our shared brokenness. She wasn't perfect, but she wanted both of us to know peace.

To her credit, Mom sent me letters weekly that included clippings, quotes, and her analyses of her dreams. Always on a quest for spiritual filling, she changed her beliefs as often as she changed clothes. But with each new shift, she exuded an optimism and hope that caught me in her passion. Mom's letters described her most recent insights into her behavior during my young life, or she would be full of advice about my present circumstances. Having abandoned me as a child, she now actively engaged with me regularly. It threw me off-center.

She sent me the following letter two years after she attended therapy with me.

3/28/81

My dearest Patricia,

I'm sitting here looking at your picture in the hall. I see your sad eyes and realize how much I rejected you when you were little. I did the best I knew how at the time. But it still didn't stop the hurt you have felt. For thirteen years, you were rejected. You used to cry when you saw that picture of the little abandoned baby sitting by the railroad track in China. I think subconsciously, you felt you were left alone too.

To make things worse, when at the dinner table, when you would not eat, your father used to say, "Eat! Those poor children in China don't have anything to eat." Thereby making you feel guilty.

When I go square dancing, I think, "I wish Patsy were here so she could enjoy this fantastic fun!"

How can I be happy when I think you are not happy, my darling daughter, whom I love more than anyone else in the world? Please let me try to undo the hurt I have caused you.

I have read books and more books, joined churches, and studied Edgar Cayce, Rosicrucianism, science of mind, etc. The books explained things intellectually, and I understood, but my old feelings of aloneness and unworthiness still existed. You can read and know the Bible intellectually, but it doesn't do any good unless you practice. If you had a book about exercise, knew the book, and read it every day, you would have no benefit to your body. Same with meditation.

I discovered the meditation tape by R. Masters. I practiced it. I listened to the tape deck every morning starting in 1970. Finally, after years, I am learning to be alone—to be my own person.

> *Meditation is a way to form the habit of being still long enough to find your inner self. It will be difficult at first, Patsy, because when you try to concentrate, your mind will be full of things you will do for the day.*
>
> *It's a long, slow process, like a grain of sand each day. But by six months, you will notice a perceptible difference deep within you! Won't you please try this so I can feel that I have done my best to undo the hurt I have caused you in the past?*
>
> *Love you,*
> *Mom*

These letters and our conversations often gave me hope that she would truly understand and nurture me. I realized she had seen my hardship with Dan long before I could admit it to anyone else—most certainly to myself. It was because of her insight and her desire to help me that she instigated joining the meeting with Dr. Jim. Reflecting on a follow-up session, my mother ended one letter like this:

> *I thought Dr. Jim made you feel guilty about Dan. Is he helping you or Dan? Let's look at this guilt. A person feels guilty because he or she is not being the real happy, sparkling being God planned. It is covered over by fear.*

My mother's actions gave me the courage to stop seeing Dr. Jim soon after that world-shifting session. The anguish of my floundering marriage consumed any joy I had known. Instead of counseling, I'd visit Mom and her husband, Paul, in Long Beach. I packed up my dog Queenie, a mutt with some Shepherd in her—and my sadness about Dan—and headed south for about an hour.

Mom loved to play with our two dogs, Mona and Queenie. Watching them, I could laugh a little. Mom was caring because I was a mess. Much to my surprise, I discovered that Mom was capable of empathy toward animals and me when my pain was extreme enough for her to notice. Watching the dogs play together and listening to Mom describe her newest insight gave me a short reprieve from the tears that often flowed when I was alone.

> *The anguish of my floundering marriage consumed any joy I had known.*

In reality, I traveled with a box of Kleenex and cried all the way there and back, having a few short hours to enjoy the dogs and be distracted by Mom and Paul's banter. Paul and I had a decent, although not particularly close, relationship. He loved to play the ponies; sometimes, I would go with them to the track. He enjoyed Mom, and he was good to her. They stayed together longer than she'd been with anyone else.

As the years passed, Paul's health declined. Mom couldn't take proper care of him anymore, and we moved him into a facility. He became frail, and his breathing labored. One morning, I called Mom to check in. "How are you doing today, Mom?"

"Honey, I'm at the beach now, walking Mona."

"Great! How is Paul today?"

"He's dead, Pat."

I was shocked, sad, and confused. She was out walking Mona on the beach!?

"You didn't think to call me?"

"There was nothing you could do, Patsy." Mom placed the fine line between crisis and calm in a different spot than me. Her ability to disconnect from reality countered my pragmatic view.

Paul's passing hit me harder than it might have had I not gotten into the routine of seeing him weekly. His death turned Mom's world upside down. It left her without a rudder and a companion. It was natural for her to rely more on me.

We talked about books we read. I took Mom to church with me occasionally. I wanted to trust her. But, despite her intelligence and attempts at making amends, she couldn't maintain stability. Having had a series of minor heart attacks and soaring blood pressure, she self-medicated more with alcohol. My mother's drinking triggered some wild mood swings and unpredictable behavior for her.

One impulsive decision she made before Paul passed was to move up to Ventura and then farther north, closer to where Allie and his family lived. She wanted to be nearer to her grandchildren. She took off, not knowing whether her son, his wife, or their children wanted to include her in their lives like she had hoped. Never happy, wherever she was, dissatisfaction and self-created chaos were always with her. The welcome news: while Mom was living away, I had a reprieve from being her frequent rescuer and caregiver. It wasn't as if my life was in order.

We Were Alike

Aunt Gertrude and I had stayed in touch over the years through cards, photographs, letters, and occasional phone calls. She was the voice of stability in my life, a wise counsel. My aunt refrained from being critical of my mother. It wasn't proper, and I suspect she knew on some level that it was not helpful for me to feel like I had to choose between them. But I think Aunt Gertrude also knew she had been the mother I needed when I was young.

Our calls were usually in the afternoon, so I knew something was wrong when I heard her voice on the line after dinner.

"Patsy, Alvar is very sick. I don't think he's going to last much longer." Aunt Gertrude's voice was soft and sad.

"Oh, Aunt Gertrude, I'm so sorry!" That must have been a massive a blow to my aunt, as she and Uncle Alvar were both struggling with cancer. I feared that when one of them died, the other would follow soon after.

"Would you come out here?" Her voice cracked. "I mean, after he's gone. I really want to see you."

"Of course I will, Aunt Gertrude. I will. You can count on it."

A couple of months later, my cousin Marilyn called with the news that her father had died. I made arrangements to get to Ohio for the funeral and to spend some time with her and Aunt Gertrude. I was shocked to see Aunt Gertrude—frail and thin from her fight with liver cancer. Where did the time go? It was 1982, and it had been several years since I'd seen her.

I put my arms around her, and despite how much she had changed physically, it felt like I was home. We cried for a moment or two and then sat down. Marilyn brought us some tea, and we caught up. I stayed in the guest room for the next week. Marilyn worked during the day, so Aunt Gertrude and I had time to talk, just the two of us. I realized that Aunt Gertrude and I hadn't had a lot of one-on-one conversations over the years. I left Ohio when I was a teenager, and it wasn't until after I had Eric that I realized the value of having more connection with my aunt. We'd talked on the phone, but Uncle Alvar was in the room with her, so the conversations were more about the latest events. But now, with Uncle Alvar gone, we had time for just the two of us. It gave me the opportunity to ask her something I'd always wanted to know.

"Why did you take me in, Aunt Gertrude? All those years ago?"

She looked over at me with love in her eyes, "Oh, Patsy. How could I not?" She looked away as if trying to choose her words carefully. "One afternoon when you were about one, your dad was at work. I heard you, through the duplex wall, abruptly start screaming at the top of your lungs. It wasn't your typical cry. I could tell you were in trouble.

"I ran out our back door and into your house. Betty was asleep on the couch, completely unaware of your distress. The cries were coming from your room, so I grabbed the door and realized I could not open it—that she had locked you in. You started walking early and exploring everything. When you couldn't get out of the door, you must have climbed up on the chest of drawers and pulled it over on top of yourself."

"Really?" I hadn't heard this story before. "Was I hurt?"

She shook her head. "No, thank the good Lord. It hit up against the bed frame, and there was a little space for you. But you were trapped and screaming."

"I must have been terrified." I felt the pain of trauma in my chest as she spoke.

"Uncle Alvar got a crowbar and got the door open. I scooped you up and calmed you down. It took a lot to wake up Betty. I don't know if she'd taken some medication or was drinking—"

"Grandma Davis told me she came over a few times and heard me crying while mom seemed to be in some kind of trance."

She frowned. "I don't want to speak badly about your mother. I really don't. And when she and Al first married, we were all quite pleased. She was so lively and, well, bigger than life. She brought Al so much joy. But they married before they got to know each other. Betty had severe mood swings that Al didn't know anything about. She would get so depressed she would sit alone for hours. She seemed so terrified of life and tried to run away. Then she'd up and disappear, leaving you alone."

She sat back for a moment and sipped her tea. "Did anyone tell you about the fence your dad built around your yard?"

I shook my head no. "I do remember that we had a small fence that went all the way around our side of the duplex."

She nodded. "There wasn't one on our side. Did you notice that?"

"Yes, and we got a dog!"

"That's because your dad was afraid that Betty wouldn't take proper care of you while he was at work and that you'd wander off into the street."

My eyes got big.

"So, he built that fence around your yard so that if you did get outside without her knowing it, you'd be safe in the yard."

I remembered Dusty and how he stayed by my side all the time. "Dad did all this because he knew…" My stomach ached, and I shook my head. "Mom…" I hardly knew what to say.

Reaching over, she patted my hand. "Your mother wasn't capable of being a mother to you. Maybe she can now, but she couldn't then. When Al went into the Navy, I heard you crying, and I went in and picked you up and brought you to our side of the duplex. Your mother just sat on the couch as if nothing was happening."

"Didn't Mom protest?"

She shook her head no. "I think she was relieved. The next thing we knew, another family moved in. She had rented out their side of the duplex, and we rarely saw her."

"What a burden I must have been."

The smile that came across my aunt's face was breathtaking. "You were so smart and interested in everything. Now, it was a challenge keeping you occupied. You'd get into mischief if you didn't have something to do. But I loved your curiosity and determination."

"You were the first mother I ever knew, Aunt Gertrude. Thank you for rescuing me. And for enjoying me."

"You helped me through a rough time when Marilyn was born, Alvar went to war, and Mom was ill. You know your Gramma Stroberg loved you so much."

You were the first mother I ever knew, Aunt Gertrude. Thank you for rescuing me.

"Remember the white apron she always wore? She always had a hanky in the pocket."

"I do." We both got lost in our memories.

"If I close my eyes, I can still feel the ease of sitting on Gramma's lap with her thin arms around me."

"I know I'm missing Alvar and dealing with my health issues, but Patsy, you have been through so much in your life."

"Thank you again, Aunt Gertrude. I'm glad I am here."

"You are a strong woman, Pat."

"Do you really think so?" As an adult, Aunt Gertrude had never praised me like that before.

"I do. And do you want to know what else I think?"

"Oh, yes."

"I think you and I are very much alike."

With that, we laughed so hard I thought I'd cry. Honestly, I think I did cry a little. She was the kindest, most loving, and stable person I'd ever known. She made others feel welcome—she made me feel welcome. How wonderful to hear she thought we shared the same attributes. There was no one in the world I'd rather be compared to than my Aunt Gertrude.

Disappointment and Loss at Forty-Three

I was about to turn forty-three, a year I had waited for since I was ten, when I had seriously contemplated killing myself by jumping out of my bedroom window. Somehow, I came to believe that my misery in life would be cut short when I turned forty-three. Why did I choose that year? I have no idea. It wasn't as if I intended to hurt myself in the future. But I thought that I was going to die sometime after I turned forty-three and before my forty-fourth birthday.

January 3, 1983, my forty-third birthday, came and went. I was disappointed that I was still among the living. I sunk deeper into the darkness around me—suffering from menopause and marital issues. I was waiting for something to happen that would save me from the pain. I did have a novel feeling. It showed up as I was standing at the Southwest Airlines ticket counter. I felt anger bubble up within me. It stayed with me until I was home. I couldn't define it, but I felt it. Frozen inside for so much of my life, I finally started to feel the ache of the deep wounds I carried internally. This compounded the depression I knew too well.

But nothing happened, month after month. I didn't get sick. I wasn't in a car accident. The days slowly rolled by, one miserable sunrise after another. And then, one day, my life spun out of control. Yet, Eric was my sole blessing.

Dan and I had bought a small home on Covina Hills Road as an income property. We rented it to a nice family with a daughter named Liz. They were good renters, and we became friends over the years. When Liz graduated from high school, we'd been supportive by offering her a position in our company. One day, Dan abruptly told me that he was moving out of our home but didn't tell me why. One might think he'd find another residence. But instead, he moved a bed into his office at our shop!

On a Saturday morning, Eric and his girlfriend, Kate, came by to take me to breakfast. We dropped by our business office, knowing Dan was staying there. Eric said his dad had a cold, so I suggested we check and see if he wanted some food. We drove to the office.

Kate opened the office door without knocking, and Eric and I trailed behind. We all came to a fast stop when we found Dan and Liz in the makeshift office bed. My heart broke. I'd never seen him with another woman, let alone in bed with one. Plus, it was Liz! Instantly, I realized everyone at our company knew of this arrangement but me.

I stormed into my office and packed up my work papers; I left the building like I was gathering the pieces of my heart. I worked from home from that day forward, no longer being able to face that horrid man or our employees with the humiliation and pain of the situation.

When I told my mother about Liz and Dan, she said I needed to get another therapist—one that could help me this time. I followed her advice and found a rather ordinary-looking woman named Vanessa. She was anything but the run-of-the-mill counselor. Not only did she listen to me and empower me to disconnect from Dan, but she also taught me the principles of psychology, helped me set boundaries, and showed me how to better use the support my friends and family could offer. I'd plead with her, "Fix me!"

She saw me as a whole person. "You're not crazy, Pat," she'd reassure me repeatedly. She gave me the courage to be vulnerable and feel the hurt.

"And what about Dan?" I asked Vanessa one afternoon.

"He is deeply wounded and has no self-awareness. Dan is a master of projection."

"What's that?"

"Instead of seeing himself clearly, he believes that other people are doing to him what he is doing to them."

I sat back for a moment. "I don't understand."

"What is the last thing he accused you of doing, Pat?"

"That I was sleeping around and couldn't be trusted."

She smiled. "Are you sleeping around?"

"Of course not!"

As if leading a small child to a treasure, she asked, "And who is sleeping around?"

The light bulb went on. "Dan is!"

She nodded. "He constantly accuses you of doing what he is doing, thinking what he is thinking, or wanting what he wants."

"That's right! I can see that now!"

Vanessa sat back in her high-back chair. "And what does Dan want, Pat?"

The bottom of my stomach dropped as I realized the answer. "Dan wants everything. Other women, the business, the money—"

"And complete control over you."

"Yes, he wants that most of all. Vanessa, if you can't fix the marriage, fix me."

"Let's help you heal," she said.

We had many sessions, disentangling Dan's lies and squelching words that had suffocated my true self. It was grueling work. Vanessa was patient, honest, and safe as she guided me out of my emotional maze because of his damaging statements, control, and rejection. She beamed at me one day with so much love. "Pat, you are perfect. Just as you are, you are perfect." Her words pivoted me toward a new life, a new freedom.

Insights about Dan dovetailed insights about Mom. Vanessa explained Mom's mental illness. Vanessa used the term manic-depressive, which I'd heard of, and the new term bipolar. Without medication, my mother would never be emotionally stable; what was available then was just being developed.

Discovering that Mom had some capacity to self-reflect and see me as a separate human being she had hurt was something I could embrace. But that didn't change the fact that Mom was and would always be a drama queen and chaos maker.

This piece of knowledge helped me not be as irritated by her antics. I looked to a future with her moods swinging, disregarding others, from one side of the emotional spectrum to the other. Vanessa ushered me wisely through the confusing labyrinth of coping with Mom.

> *"Patsy, why didn't you stop me?" I thought long and hard. "Mom, no one can stop a tank."*

I had to accept that each nugget of support Mom offered to me was wrapped in an emotional explosion, whether extreme elation or despair. For example, she would spend money wildly during her manic episodes and then ask me, "Patsy, why didn't you stop me?"

I thought long and hard about that. "Mom, no one can stop a tank."

I explained to Vanessa that my dad had always been a smoker. "When I was growing up, many of the adults in my life smoked. As the news spread that smoking was so dangerous to our health, most people curbed their smoking or stopped altogether, especially around children and others. My father never quit. I remember him always having a cough. We got used to it, and when he finally went to see the doctor, he was diagnosed with end-stage emphysema."

"Pat, there is so much loss in your life right now," Vanessa said.

"It's all such a blow to me. Cancer runs strong on the Stroberg side of the family. Most of my father's siblings have one type of cancer or another. Dad was diagnosed six months after Aunt Gertrude, and the thought of losing both of them is breaking me."

Around Thanksgiving 1983, Dad, Aunt Gertrude, and I talked on the phone. Aunt Gertrude was in great pain, and Dad and I knew that she had just days to live. Dad was on the kitchen phone, and I got on the one in the master bedroom. We all talked about everything but what was happening to them.

"Aunt Gertrude, you take care." My voice quivered.

"Gertrude, keep comfortable," Dad managed to say. At the end of the call, we were all in tears. I knew that that was the last time the three of us would talk and the last time we would hear her voice.

Aunt Gertrude embodied the goodness of Ohio, God, and family always. She was home for me. Her death on December 7th eroded more ground under my feet. She was my primary object, my mother, during my first years of life. She was safety, love, and calm wrapped up in a person. The bond I felt with her was rivaled only by Dad; their personalities were so similar. Throughout my life, this brother and sister team cushioned the chaos and insecurity brought by my mother and then Dan.

As 1983 came to a close and my forty-fourth birthday approached in January, it looked like the fantasy escape from my pain would not be fulfilled. I was still physically alive but felt dead inside—defeated and deflated. Life without Aunt Gertrude left me untethered. Dad's illness was progressing, and I braced myself for the most devastating loss yet. How would I carry on without the two anchors that had sustained me my entire life? Miserable, disappointed, and overtaken by despair, I cried out repeatedly, "Help me, Lord."

This Woman Is in Charge

Through January and into February of 1984, I focused what little energy I had on spending as much time as possible with my dad. I was so glad he and Alice decided the Oregon cold wasn't for them and returned to Covina after only two years there.

I'd ride my bike to his house every day. We'd share coffee and talk about the news. It was also a great help to Alice, who was quickly overwhelmed by his illness and all it entailed. She was pretty dependent on my father, and when his abilities declined, she became increasingly fragile and agitated. My visits allowed her time for herself.

Dad was as supportive as he could be, ever delighted in the time we could spend together. Those days when I was so low, he was a frail older man, but his love for me was evident. Dad was an anchor to me, especially at that point. Visiting him was a regular ritual; I will always cherish those memories.

In February 1984, my father took a turn for the worse and transitioned to a convalescent home. I got word from the facility that I needed to get there as soon as possible. I grabbed my keys and walked out my front door. To my dismay, Dan was walking up the driveway.

"I can't talk now, Dan. Dad is dying."

He halted and said, "I'll drive you."

Perhaps I was surprised that he would help me, or maybe it was the anguish, but I dropped my guard and got into his car. We drove in silence to the facility.

When we arrived at Sunrise Convalescent, as I was practically running into the lobby of the facility, Dad's nurse approached me in the hall and said that he had already passed. Stunned and dizzy, I asked, "Is Alice in there?" I had assumed that Alice was at the hospital with him.

The nurse shook her head. "No, ma'am. When the doctor told her he was about to pass, she started crying and left."

"She didn't even call me. I would have been here." Hot tears of anger stung my eyes. "Did Dad die alone?"

"We were here with him, Pat, but no family."

Alice allowed her fear of hospitals and death to overwhelm her. I was devastated and deeply disappointed in Alice for not letting me know he was in his last moments. I hadn't been there to hold my dad's hand—to tell him goodbye.

"Well, I need to see him." Turning toward his room to get to my dad before he was taken away, Dan grabbed me by the arm. He was white as a sheet. "Don't go in now, Pat. He's dead." Dan's voice shook. I paused and then walked away with Dan.

One of the biggest regrets I have in life is that I didn't defy him and go into the room by myself. But once again, I acquiesced to Dan's pressure. I turned away and never got to see him one last time and say goodbye. No matter the cost, I seemed unable to stand up to Dan.

I was brokenhearted and drinking to escape. The gaping hole of grief swallowed me whole.

I wrote in my journal, "The room where I keep my disappointments is overflowing. I can't take it anymore."

Perhaps the only bright spot in my life was that the divorce was initiated. It was an agonizing reality. Little did I know that divorcing Dan would be nearly as hard as being married to him.

My first lawyer was useless in advocating for me, while Dan and his attorney took every opportunity to negate my contribution to the business's success. They insisted that the company's value was the combination of the machinery we owned and Dan's skills. His legal counsel discounted all the financial management I provided, and my work was wholly overlooked.

After one particularly brutal meeting, I told my attorney I was finished. I needed out. I told him to draw up papers saying I would sell my interest in the company for $100,000. I had to include legal language that stated I "gifted" him the house he bought for $5,000.

On that late spring night, I fell onto my bed as I often did, pleading with God in anguish. "I just want to die, to go away." I was still deeply disappointed that I was forty-four and alive—living a miserable life.

When I prayed, I didn't usually get a response. But on that unique evening, I moved from lying down to kneeling. Elbows on the bed and my head bowed over folded hands, I experienced an angel on my shoulder. God's presence came into the room, and I knew I wasn't alone in my despair. I felt comfort, warmth, and love, which transformed me. The words Mom had written to me in a note flooded my mind. *A person feels guilty because he is not being the real happy, sparkling being God planned. It is covered over by fear.*

I didn't have to be afraid any longer. The fears and burdens of Dan, Mom, Dad, finances, and the sad story of my childhood didn't have to sink me. That night, I realized how I lived my life was *my* choice. I was not a victim of any of these! Empowered, I sat up and said out loud, "I don't want to die, God! *I want to live!*" My body surged with energy.

"I am going to fight for this life!" I pounded on the bed through tears. "No one is going to step on me anymore." Exhausted, I fell into a peaceful sleep, and rather than waking up several times during the night with anxiety, the next time I opened my eyes, the phone rang. It was morning.

I reached for the phone on my bedside table, knowing Dan would be on the other end of the line. Panic swept over me. *Hours ago, I gave Dan the control he wanted over me—before I decided to fight for what is rightfully mine! Now, what am I going to do?*

Dan's angry voice blared from the receiver. "You bitch! I will not accept these terms! How dare you state that you are 'gifting' my house to me. The house is mine. You can't give me something that I already own." Before I could respond, the sound of ripping paper on his end spoke volumes. "I've torn up the papers, Pat!" He hung up.

Joy filled my heart. Relief. Dan had no idea what he had done. I'd given him *everything*—my identity, my interest in the company that was as much mine as it was his, and my will to live. He had won, but he still wasn't satisfied. With my newfound strength and immense relief from Dan's refusal of my offer, I got out of bed and headed to the shower. Sensing an angel on my shoulder, I confidently said to no one but me, "I'll never make that mistake again."

I had been afraid all my life. And when I looked back over the years, it was no wonder. I thought the only way to escape the terrors of life was to leave this world. But deep inside, I had always had a will to live. I had to reach rock bottom, into the darkest corner of my being, to find that self-love and determination. And when I landed in that honest, vulnerable space, God was there to lead me back to the light.

I stared in the bathroom mirror and saw a different woman. I looked different. There wasn't that same fear in my eyes. As a little girl, I'd somehow decided that my forty-third year would be a game-changer. I expected to die physically but didn't; instead, I confronted my fear and was transformed into someone new. So, I had been on target all along.

It was indisputable that my decisions would be based on anxiety, not on wisdom and clear thinking when I was fearful. I often heard my mother's anxious voice in my head. "Oh, Patsy. Be careful! You could make a huge mistake and lose everything!" But I heard a new voice that told me to name my fear and realize I had power over it. I could live without anxiousness if I let go of self-doubt and listened to the angel on my shoulder.

> "I looked different. There wasn't that same fear in my eyes."

I would no longer live like a victim, giving away my power and letting fear lead me. The enormity of this revelation swept over me. Gratitude to God filled my heart.

While I had decided to fight for myself, I had no idea how to do that. No one in my family modeled proper ways to deal with conflict. On the contrary, I saw people exploding or running away and withdrawing. Like my father, I had drawn inward and fell into depression. I wasn't interested in taking lessons from my mother and Dan. So, it took time, sessions with Vanessa, and slow steps to gain confidence and find my voice.

I believe that when people are emotionally clear about who they are and what they want and are spiritually aligned with what is true, power is set into motion, supplying them with unexpected opportunities. I'd seen it in other people's lives but had never experienced it. My declaration that "I want to live" was uttered in privacy. I believe that my decision reverberated through my life and released a new vibration in my world.

It all started with taking one step, firing my current attorney—I'm not sure if he was negligent or incompetent—and hiring Joel Tucker, a brilliant and effective negotiator. I was ready to fight for myself through the divorce with his help. Little did I know that a door was about to open for me—a possibility I had never imagined, let alone tried to pursue.

Being smart and cunning, Dan slowly took my name off our accounts, undermined my reputation among our employees, and, unbeknownst to me, plotted to cheat me out of a fair price for my company buyout. Month after month, Dan set up his trap.

In the summer of 1985, my mortgage check bounced, and though my mother's words surfaced, "Oh Patsy, be careful," I could speak more for myself. I called Dan immediately.

"Dan, my mortgage check bounced. I need access to the bank statements."

"No."

"Then send me the pink slip to my car."

"No!" Click.

I was in Tucker's office the next day. He reminded me that I owned fifty percent of the company and could call a board meeting. I'd forgotten I had power I wasn't using. And so I followed his advice and called a board meeting for September 10, 1985—one of the most important days of my life.

We met in a conference room at the Embassy Suites in West Covina. Tucker and I got there early so I could pick my seat—in the middle of the table to see everyone. If I had that to do over again, I'd have taken the seat at the head of the table, but I was still learning. We had a stenographer to record the proceedings.

On my right was Bob Williams, the special counsel representing me and the corporation, and on my left was Tucker. I took a deep breath, trying to stay calm as I waited to see Dan walk through the door. Only he didn't.

Instead, his new Los Angeles corporate attorney, Gary Manfred, walked in, his massive build filling the door as he entered. Behind him came Dan's divorce lawyer and a few people I hadn't met before. No one explained Dan's absence, and I didn't ask.

I spoke first. "This meeting is called to order at ten-o-five on September tenth, nineteen-eight-five—"

Manfred cut me off. "Dan is quite ill, and I refused to allow him to attend today's meeting."

I did my best not to show any concern, but panic was at the gate. Why did I even care? I knew he had heart issues. Doctors wouldn't even let him take a treadmill test a while back. Manfred continued, looking directly at me. "Dan intends to discontinue any involvement in this business whatsoever and turn the reins over to you."

Silence filled the room. I breathed deeply, trying to exude calm strength instead of fretfulness. I'd expected Dan to offer me a meager price for buying me out of the company, but it had never occurred to me that he would provide for me to buy him out. Never. I was stunned.

Bob Williams realized I had been blind-sided and called for a short recess. Shocked, Williams, Tucker, and I went into the adjoining room for privacy. Tucker was elated. "He's going to give the business to you!"

Refusing to feel hope, I shook my head. "He has a plan. He thinks I will run the business into the ground so he can humiliate me and then repurchase it for even less money."

Williams nodded with a huge smile on his face. "Yes, that's what he thinks you'll do. He's overplaying his hand. Pat, we all know that you kept the company financially afloat."

"He's the tool maker," I insisted. "I just did the office work."

Tucker and Williams grinned at each other. "Pat, this is your chance," Tucker said. "We're behind you. Show Dan that he has completely underestimated you."

And then it hit me—a sense of power I'd never known. I was ready for battle, and the opposition had significantly miscalculated. Taking a deep breath, I felt adrenaline pulse through my body. "Yes! Let's do this!"

We marched back into the room, although my feet couldn't feel the floor, and negotiated the price and financing terms. I had entered the negotiation with the goal of getting the pink slip to my Jetta and a buyout package I could afford. But an hour later, I left the room as the company's sole owner!

Things Turn Around

While Dan dragged his feet finalizing the divorce, I joined the Great Expectations dating service. I soon met a man named Bill. While he was tall and handsome like Dan, as a person, he was everything that Dan was not—kind, analytical, supportive, and loving. While dating, he came to the house, helped with household repairs, and cleaned up all the neglected tasks—so much had gone to disrepair during the darkness of the divorce. I was worried I was using him. "Pat, I will tell you if I feel used. It's what friends are for, and I am enjoying myself!

"I love your straightforwardness, independence, and competence," Bill said. I was the complete opposite of who I used to be! Dan never said anything affirming to me. Bill taught me about setting boundaries by respecting me and clarifying where issues stemmed from.

We had fun together. We laughed, cooked, cleaned, went out dancing, and talked many a night away. In counseling, Vanessa told me, "Bill upsets your reality because he gives to you instead of taking." I was like a dry and empty well that took in every drop of nurturance, love, and joy Bill offered. I was cautioned not to move too quickly. To guard my heart. To be afraid. But I chose to open myself instead. Bill and I fell in love and married a year after our first date.

The night before I returned to the company after a three-year absence, I was ready, exhilarated, and worried. My mind couldn't settle down. I was agitated, and my stomach ached.

Bill said, "Pat, you can handle this."

"I know Dan has said horrible things about me to so many people there, especially the management." I reached over and took an antacid and a few sips of water. "I can't stand this sick feeling in my gut. It reminds me of when everyone blamed me, although I was innocent."

Bill wasn't clear on what memory I was referencing. He patiently listened to my retelling of what happened.

"Carol, Sally, and I were ninth graders, and Agatha was in the eighth. She was always trying to push her way into our group. She was younger and kind of odd. But she lived on my street, so I talked to her."

"You still show kindness like that, Pat." Bill kissed me, and we repositioned so he could see my face as I shared this story from my life.

"However, if my friends and I could avoid her, we did. We were only fifteen.

"The four of us were walking home from school, and, as usual, I walked a bit ahead of the group. I heard a shrill scream, turned around, and was horrified to see my friends attacking Agatha with their lipsticks. They slashed them on her face, jacket, and books. The two of them took off running for home.

"'My jacket! My dad's new jacket!' Agatha cried.

"I was in shock. 'Agatha, are you okay?' I helped her pick up her books. There were lines of lipstick everywhere, especially on the leather-sleeved jacket she was wearing. And she couldn't stop crying."

Bill checked in with me. "Your stomach calming down?"

"Maybe a little. Anyway, I helped Agatha get home. I was stunned that my friends would act in such a mean way.

"Once I got home, I said hi to Allie and got us both a snack. Carol called and asked me not to tell her father what had happened because he would beat her. I asked, 'Why did you and Sally do this? Why didn't you tell me your plan first?' Without hesitating, Carol said, 'Because, Patsy, we knew you would try to stop us!'"

Getting animated as he listened, Bill, an enthusiastic husband, said, "Pat! I agree with them. I know you'd have stopped them. You have such an innate sense of justice."

"You're right. That sense of justice has always guided me.

"Back to the story, Agatha's father showed up in the evening, madder than hell, waving the ruined jacket in the air. I thought to myself, 'Why is he here? I haven't done anything wrong.' I guess I was guilty by association, by hearsay. Then Carol's mom showed up at our door in an attempt to get at the truth.

"Dad said, 'Patsy, knock on the bathroom door and tell your mom to get out of the tub, now!'"

"I gestured for him to hurry.

"The whole house erupted into chaos again, this time everyone talking over each other. There were so many loud voices and accusations while Dad, Allie, and I quietly watched.

"Finally, Dad had something to say, but not to them. Looking straight at me, he asked, 'Pat, did you hurt Agatha and put lipstick on this jacket?' I looked sadly at the beautiful, now damaged, jacket and remembered the horror of her scream. I glanced at all the adult faces, quiet now and staring at me, and I felt sick. 'No, Dad. No, I didn't!'

"There was a cyclone of questions and negotiations between my mom and Agatha's dad about the cost of the coat and some consequences. They started blaming me, but I told them I was innocent, and my dad listened to me and believed me."

Bill tightened his embrace. "Pat, you are amazing. You are ready to return to the company. You will set things right."

"I'm glad the judge had favor on me. I'm going back to work tomorrow!"

"Let's get some sleep." Bill was asleep before I could reach over and turn off the light.

The next day, I boldly walked into the office I had fled in humiliation three years prior. The managers, including my son, Eric, stared in disbelief. I knew they knew the details of my personal life, and, as a woman, I was breaking the glass ceiling by becoming the female owner of a tooling and molding manufacturing company. The divorce was concluded—finally. No longer did I have to shift my days according to Dan's moods, control, and business style.

That's not to say it was easy for a woman in the 1980s to run a manufacturing company. I was very well connected to manufacturing companies in the greater Los Angeles area, and there wasn't one with a woman at the helm.

Dan had set up a number of traps to aid in my failure, like telling our managers that I intended to fire everyone on the first day. He also told the customers that I wouldn't honor the contracts. And Dan had created a toxic environment of sexual impropriety, fostering sexual harassment of female employees. There was a lot to clean up. But I got the company! I was energized and felt hope. I was giddy with the lack of oppression. I'm sure my feet didn't touch the ground for at least three weeks.

Running full throttle, I took the reins of our company. It was a dance to regain the trust of the managers and leads at our shop. Dan had tainted my character and done his best to sabotage the company's success under my leadership. I was just elated to return to my office after almost three years. Surveying the production numbers and finances, I observed, listened, and cleaned up.

I worked hard to soar, but I did it. The company continued to succeed and to grow. More significantly, I opened myself to healing. Disentangling myself from Dan was a process that continued long after the 1985 divorce. His strangling words, humiliating tactics, and conflicting messages were hurdles I cleared again and again as I grew in my leadership role.

Fred Purdy, a business professor from Mount San Antonio Junior College, visited the company when I first took over. After I made my changes, Fred returned to check on me and walk through the plant. "Pat, I like the new manner the place has. All the people are smiling. It feels productive here." He was right.

The tone of the company had changed under my leadership. Just because Dan had been awful didn't mean I had to be. There were struggles and stresses, but no more rage. I created a work climate that put a stop to sexual harassment, disrespect, and intimidation. An atmosphere of reasonableness and mutual respect was now present.

I thought back to when Lillian, my first boss and mentor, had reminded me over lunch, "Dan was never ambitious; you were, Pat." I could agree with her now. Before, I was locked into the man being the one in charge, better suited than a woman. My empowerment and building success with the company proved otherwise. Discovering two ongoing sexual harassment situations, I quickly fired the night shift managers—who had been instigating the harassment—and created a "no tolerance" atmosphere. Justice was clearly part of the company climate. My life had transformed. Not only was I in charge, I was a change agent.

> *I worked hard to soar, but I did it.*

The company I co-founded became a multi-million-dollar business, employing hundreds of people over the years. Once I said "yes" to life, my direction changed.

Vanessa, my therapist of many years, my mom, and a handful of friends walked me through the transition from oppression to liberation. With "successful" and "strong leader" now describing me, I joined a group of peers—aptly named TEC, The Executives Committee—business executives who met monthly for over thirteen years to teach, challenge, and support each other. New buildings, remodels, increased employees, and diversity in our product line were all big achievements. I traveled the world and enjoyed life for the first time.

Enough Isn't Enough for Everyone

In 1990, I met Dr. Gladys McGary, a living saint who changed my life. My first encounter with her was hearing her speak about holistic health at a conference sponsored by the Edgar Cayce Institute. Her words inspired and intrigued me—the blending of mind, body, and spirit resonated. At seventy-three, she exuded health, wisdom, and a life force I wanted to know and have for myself.

I stood in line to meet her, curious if she could help me with my physical issues in menopause, chronic bloating, and digestive distress. I was in pain and also highly fatigued all the time. My regular doctors couldn't find anything wrong with me. In my brief encounter with her at the conference, I shared enough of my story for her to look me square in the face. She lovingly stated, "Pat, I am unsure how I will help you. I do know I will tell you the truth." Her frank response was coated in empathy. I had hope begin to emerge within me.

A daughter of medical missionaries in India, Dr. Gladys had known from a young age that she wanted to be a doctor. She had spent her life caring for thousands in her medical practice and traveling in the United States and abroad with her skills and message. This humble mother of eight, speaker, and author embodied the healing she offered others. I wanted to learn from her, experience healing, and grow. In 1991, I traveled to her clinic in Scottsdale, Arizona to be assessed, treated, and guided by this Western medical doctor who embraced holistic practices. Once there, a vibrant and healthy seventy-three-year-old Dr. Gladys walked toward me and gave me a hug. I liked doctors who hugged you. (If she had dyed her hair, she would have looked fifty!)

At my first visit to her medical practice, I was applauded for my existing exercise regimen, decreased salt intake, and diet. I learned I had Candida, a wheat allergy, and I would have been much sicker if I hadn't been a few steps ahead already. Soon, I was set up on a new regimen of garlic, oregano, no fungi, and a myriad of supplements.

I felt so hopeful when I left for California. I finally found a doctor who would treat all of me and not just one symptom. After years of suffering from physical maladies, my body started to heal. So did the rest of me. I finally knew more good days than bad. *Now I can get better.*

For the next several years, my life stabilized into a routine of work and family. Bill and I achieved a level of love and intimacy that I'd never experienced with Dan. He supported and advised me well in my work and attended church with me—a special gift.

We were at church one Sunday, sitting in the choir loft. My mind was not on the service because I was worried about making payroll. My sleep had been troubled all that week, worrying about the problems at the shop. Just as I would resolve one issue, another would emerge. The accounts receivable and payroll were constantly at odds. It took me years at the company and some internal growth to stop being preoccupied with work. I was a stressed-out type A personality. Many employees depended on us, we relied on them, and all aspects of the business had to sync well each week.

As the priest shared his homily, I had a vision looking down toward the altar. Awestricken, I looked at Bill to see if he saw what I saw! He didn't. There was a cornucopia pouring out money at the front of the church. I concluded it meant the parish was well off. Then, the cornucopia moved directly above my head. I heard a voice in my head say, "You dumb shit!" It then began to pour out dollar bills on my head. I laughed inside, smiling at Bill, wishing he could see what I was experiencing.

> *I realized, then and there, the Lord was going to take care of me.*

My heart responded over and over, "Thank you, Lord!" I realized, then and there, that the Lord was going to take care of me. The extraordinary vision's message was, "Don't worry, your needs will be met." I was reminded to stop living in scarcity and instead live in faith and abundance.

Our family gatherings were so much more enjoyable with Bill. My extended family was an odd assortment. Of course, my mother was always a power to be reckoned with. But with Dan out of the picture, there was only one star and no need to compete to be the center of attention.

Alice and Mom seemed to coexist quite well, and, as my father's widow, Alice was still considered part of our clan. I tried to be angry with her for not contacting me as Dad was dying, but I knew her well. She had always relied heavily on Dad, was riddled with fear, and could not face his death. Ultimately, she was unable to cope independently and remarried almost immediately after my father died. She felt closer to us than her family, so she brought Ric, her new husband, into our fold.

Ric was a nice man, albeit a bit obsessive. His worst trait was that he didn't like dogs, and there was always at least one dog in my home. Generally, I found him to be agitating as he fussed over Alice, making sure she had whatever she needed. Alice seemed to enjoy that.

Allie and his family joined us, or we traveled north to them a few times each year to share a meal and celebrate. Eric stayed local, finished college, and used his engineering skills at our company.

Grandma Davis rounded out the group's senior members, chatty, sweet, and always in pain and relying on her walker. In the past, the tension was among my grandmother, mother, and aunt. But that dynamic changed as I became more successful, wealthier, and happier in my marriage. Aunt Evelyn expanded her jealousy to include me in her sights along with my mother. Always simmering under the surface in a slow, passive-aggressive way, it took very little to put her over the top and into attack mode. The arguments were always about money.

Grandma Davis carried a pink plastic purse with her wherever she went. One day, when she was staying with me, she opened her purse, and I saw a large roll of dollar bills. I asked, "Grandma, how much money is in that purse?"

"It's money I earned, fair and square." Grandma had been a maid for a motel near the Santa Anita Race Track for years, where many celebrities stayed when visiting the race track. She smiled and said, "You know, Desi Arnaz was always a good tipper."

I grinned. Grandma loved to tell that story. "But Grandma, how much cash are you carrying around?"

She grabbed the bundle, and we sat down and counted it together. "Grandma, there's over two thousand dollars in here!"

"I told you, Desi Arnaz was a good tipper."

"You shouldn't be carrying around this much cash. Someone will rob you."

"But I want to have this money so that if I ever go into a hospital, I can get treats for myself. And I can't put it into an account in my own name because they will decrease my social security payments."

I patted her on the shoulder. "Then I'll deposit it in a separate account in my name, and you can access it whenever you need the money."

She agreed, and a few days later, I opened the account and gave her the needed information.

Not long after this occurred, Aunt Evelyn arrived to take Grandma Davis to her house for the next couple of months. Grandma Davis showed her the banking information, and Aunt Evelyn blew up at me. "How dare you put *my* mom's money into your bank account! Are you trying to take her money?"

I was shocked at the accusation. "What are you talking about? I don't need Grandma's money. She was carrying it around in that pink purse and could be robbed. It's for her safety."

Aunt Evelyn's voice went up a notch. "I work all day and night taking care of Mom. I do her grocery shopping, get her to appointments, and…" On and on she went.

I tried to stop her and explain myself, but she kept talking over me, getting angrier by the second.

"Stop, Aunt Evelyn! You're not listening to me!" I was surprised by my intensity. She continued, so I said again, this time with greater volume, "Aunt Evelyn, you're not listening to me!"

Her mouth dropped open, shocked that I would yell at her. I was a bit shocked myself—I'd never been the recipient of my aunt's wrath before. I'd watched as she ripped Mom to shreds, but it felt entirely different being the person who was getting torn.

Aunt Evelyn stood and asked, "What did you say to me?"

I sat back in my chair.

"Maybe you're a fancy businesswoman and rich and all, and you think you're the boss of everyone because you run a big company. But you *can't* talk to me like that!"

I was upset and started crying. She sat down, and there was silence as we tried to regain our composures. After several minutes, Aunt Evelyn said, "Okay, I'm ready to listen now." *Sure you are. Now that you've put me in my place.*

After they left, I thought about what it must have been like for Mom to grow up in this family. Grandma didn't try to stop us from arguing. She certainly didn't protect me from my aunt's temper. I'd seen this happen to Mom, but it was the first time my aunt attacked me. Something broke between us that afternoon. My success threatened her, so I had become fair game.

I saw my mom in a new light—someone who had been blamed and cornered without being able to defend herself. I imagined her as a little girl with a jealous older sister and a mom who never came to her aid.

In the late 1980's, my Grandma Davis's health declined steadily. One afternoon in 1990, Grandma was taking a turn staying with Mom, and she complained of severe pain in her abdomen. Mom took her to St. Mary's Hospital in Long Beach. I went to visit her.

The doctor explained her condition. "Mrs. Davis may have a bowel obstruction, and her intestines might be twisted. She's in a lot of pain, so we're keeping her on morphine."

Sitting beside her bed, I took her hand. She was going in and out of consciousness. She pointed to the ceiling, murmuring. "Look, Patsy, do you see the little angels?"

I didn't, but I told her I did. Her face broke out in a big smile. "And look, Grandpa is coming too." Once she had fallen asleep, I kissed her on the forehead. I told her I'd be back the next day. That night, she passed away in her sleep. It was September 27, 1990.

My reaction to losing Grandma Davis was confusing to me. I believed she had tried her best to care for me as a child. As I grew up, we connected again as adults. But I also saw her as a significant player in the wounds Mom suffered and then passed on to me. It was hard not to resent her as well as miss her.

I Forgive You

I had been seeing Dr. Gladys for nine years at this point. She was my lifeline to healing—not just physically but from the trauma I'd experienced in my childhood and marriage. Dr. Gladys and Eileen, the therapists who worked with me, were wise and direct. Our sessions were long and intense, taking me deeper into my soul work.

"You realize, Pat, that you have been a caretaker and nurturer of those around you since birth. Your mom, brother, cousin, husband, and even your dad relied on you. It's time to focus on yourself by honoring the stable, dependable, and hard-working parts of you."

I agreed. "I am not nurturing myself."

"You must attend to all of your parts to heal."

It's time to take care of myself. But then my mind went blank. *How do I do that?*

The team homed in on my relationship with Mom. "You were emotionally abused by your mom," Dr. Gladys clarified. "She abandoned you. She is the primary source of these unhealthy emotional patterns."

I knew I needed to quit wasting time and get on with this soul work. I was fifty-seven years old and still trying to forgive my mother. Yes, I'd been reading and studying about emotional and spiritual health for years. My lifetime routine of daily journaling, meditating, and walking was great. Still, it undoubtedly did not address my health and well-being roadblocks. I worked hard, was successful, served the greater community, attended church, and sang in the choir weekly, but how would I achieve real internal change?

It's time to take care of myself. But then my mind went blank. How do I do that?

The catalyst for my life transformation came in the form of a women's group I worked with for ten months. I committed to meeting with six other women in Phoenix for monthly four-day intensive retreats led by Dr. Gladys and her team. At the retreat center, we had individual therapy and group processing, journaling, massage, acupuncture, meditation, psychic guidance, and healthy meals. Barbara, Stella, Nell, Rene, Dale, Janet, and I forged friendships as we bared our souls in the circle of couches and chairs and experienced release from what hindered each of us.

As an early riser, I loved walking in the desert morning's coolness and watching the Arizona sunrise. So did Dr. Gladys. Often, on the path through the property, we would share the quiet space of the colorful sky and stillness. Stopping to sit on the east-facing bench, we would watch the vista come to life. I would chat about the retreat, and she would listen intently, expecting my soul to communicate with her.

One morning, as I chattered on about my anger and depression, she spoke out. "Pat, I want you to breathe out your sadness as you walk." In the light of sunrise, her direction shifted me to actively blow away the negative parts of my life as I exhaled. To walk, move, and intentionally breathe out the baggage—just one of her many pearls.

Three months into our intensives, it was my turn to share my life story. I had the chance to reveal to the group, for an entire day, the complexity and pain of being my mother's daughter. I read the letter I'd written to Mom aloud: "You were abusive. You were neglectful. You abandoned me. I HATE YOU!" The confusion of her chaotic and selfish behaviors and the challenge of the perpetual pull of her neediness of me spewed out of me. Dr. Gladys coached me, "Don't carry animosity around with you, Pat, because it is damaging. It is time to let it go." Equipped with a forgiveness prayer I read for the next forty days, I uttered these words before the witnesses: "I forgive you, Mom."

As I spoke aloud so honestly in a circle of acceptance, I felt the release of the emotional chains I had always known. I embraced my choice to love her, with her flaws and chaos. I stopped expecting from her what I now knew she couldn't offer. I grew to understand she was a person with a story too. No longer was I at the mercy of my mother's pathology. Reflecting on my actions in the weeks after, I journaled, "Thank you, Lord. Now, I am strong; I am free. I can survive. No more internalizing the horrible."

This deep soul work impacted every part of my life. I was more open-hearted, had greater wisdom, and gained a life perspective that was far beyond survival and success. My journey of forgiveness of Mom released me in ways I can't fully convey. But internal shifts and outward steps toward more peace and acceptance tempered and unburdened me. My spiritual journey matured to be more about others than myself. I wanted to be St. Francis's "channel of peace" to others.

I was fifty-seven when I forgave my mother. She was seventy-seven. I learned that forgiveness is something that changed me. It healed me. It even changed my singing voice from alto to soprano! I had hoped, as many do, that once we forgive another person for hurting us, their behavior will change. Perhaps it does in some cases—if the other person is capable and willing to do the same level of deep soul work. While I believe my mother tried to the best of her ability, and she said "yes" to working on things intently with me, the reality was there was only so much change that occurred. I was internally unburdened and free from expectations that could never be met.

But to be truthful, my external relationship with my mother became more challenging. As she aged and her health deteriorated, she was more dependent upon my care. But the difference for me was that I had been able to release myself from the toxic bond that bound me to her for decades. The change in me was unmistakable and undeniable. Not because I was suddenly different—I was still Pat with all my strengths and shortfalls. But I no longer carried this heavy resentment and pain regarding my mother.

I didn't excuse her behavior; I forgave her, and that allowed me to live in a different spectrum of emotional options.

Mom noticed it immediately. "Pat, thank you for forgiving me." That was a beautiful sentiment, and my heart filled up. Then she added, "It's the best thing you've ever done for me!"

I smiled sadly because, as was my mother's way, she made my forgiving her all about her, not about me. But even that didn't trigger my old feelings. I knew who she was. And, despite all the damage caused and work I'd had to do to repair my heart, I accepted her. That opened her up to one more amazing experience.

Peace, Finally

Years passed, during which I chose to enjoy Mom more. I sought ways to connect beyond playing cards, drinking coffee, ventures to Desert Hot Springs or Las Vegas casinos, and our dogs. "Mom! Let's take a real trip together."

"Travel abroad? Oh, Patsy. I don't know if I could do it."

"Where do you want to go? Just name it." I silently hoped she'd say Ireland, as we loved our Irish roots. I knew her fears might keep her stateside, but I really wanted to do this.

"Pat, I want to take a cruise."

"Great, I'll stop by the travel agent tomorrow."

Mom and I sat at the kitchen table, pouring over booklets, and decided on an Alaskan cruise. We chose to leave from Seattle and settled on a handful of excursions.

"And Pat, can Evelyn come with us?" I cringed, knowing Evelyn could try my patience. But I conceded, deciding more hands on deck with Mom would be good.

I knew that a trip with Mom would include chaos. Once aboard the ship, all passengers have to attend the safety practice. I was there, but Mom and Evelyn weren't. We'd only been on board for three hours! They were not accounted for, and the steward was straightforward with me. "Your mother and aunt need to learn the safety protocol. They need to put on their life jackets and be able to meet at, let's see, the safety checkpoint forty-one on Deck Three. No one on board gets to skip this."

I was perplexed and a little worried about how I lost Mom and Evelyn. I returned to my cabin and immediately knocked on the door of our adjoining rooms. "Hey, Mom, you there?"

Mom's familiar whine greeted us through the closed door. "Oh, Pat, our cabin is so nice, and you weren't here. I decided I needed a bubble bath."

"Mom! You and Aunt Evelyn need to do the safety check. You missed it. It's mandatory."

The adjoining door was open now, and Aunt Evelyn and Mom were stretched out on their beds reading books. My mom had been in the bathtub during the safety drill and couldn't get out fast enough to get there on time.

I was exasperated, but I also laughed at the predictable absurdity of her actions. The next day was even worse. I was walking around the deck and noticed a commotion up ahead. People were circled with panicked faces and murmurings: "There must be a drill." "Maybe there's a problem?" "I'm getting my life jacket on now!" They asked my mom, "Do you know something we don't know?"

Then, Mom's shrill voice pierced through the crowd. "My daughter, Pat, said it was mandatory to put on life jackets."

Aunt Evelyn matter-of-factly reported, "And we were to practice standing at station forty-one on Deck Three."

The steward walked up and dispersed the crowd, reassuring everyone. "Everything is fine. There is no emergency or drill right now."

I looked at Mom and Aunt Evelyn incredulously. "Mom, what are you two doing?"

Simultaneously, they responded, oblivious to the spectacle they had caused. "We're practicing."

In early November 2000, Ric called me with the news. "Alice died yesterday, Pat!"

It was an expected phone call, but I was still upset to receive it. Alice and Ric had been married for fifteen years. Still sporting her dyed red hair, she was eighty-eight years old when she passed away.

"I'm so sorry, Ric."

Alice had been part of my life for decades, also having a fifteen-year marriage to my father since the 1960s. She'd been married previously, too, and had children before marrying my father. Her family wasn't overly inviting and had never accepted Ric as husband number three. I knew that Alice's children wouldn't step up, and Ric would be too overwhelmed to manage the funeral arrangements alone.

"I'll help you with the service, Ric. I know you are devastated."

"Thank you so much, Pat." He started to cry and hung up.

Thanksgiving was coming, and Alice's family refused to include Ric, so he had nowhere to go. And since he'd spent most Thanksgivings with us anyway, I invited him to our house. It was the usual group. This year, Eric included a few of his friends. Taking a break from his medical practice, Allie traveled with his family to Covina—a full house, except for Alice's empty chair.

The next day, Ric paid Bill and me a surprise visit, pulling into the driveway with his car filled with QVC purchases—an addiction of Alice's in her later years. "Do you mind if I spend the day here, Pat?" He grinned. "I have presents!" Standing at the front door with several boxes in his hands, he looked pathetic.

I was happy to invite him in. "You can come any time, Ric."

Bill laughed. "And you don't need to bring gifts." Ric lingered in the kitchen, wanting to be helpful, although he was just underfoot.

Busy still cleaning up from the big group and meal the day before, I directed Ric elsewhere. First, he helped Bill put away the extra chairs and the dining room table leaf. Then he was back in the kitchen. I whispered to Mom, "Keep Ric out of the kitchen! I can't get anything done here with him underfoot."

Mom's distinctive voice rang out as she responded to my plea. "Ric, I'd love to have someone to play cards with while Pat and Bill finish in the kitchen."

"Sure, Betty. I'll play some cards." If he had been a dog, he would have wagged his tail.

The next day, the same thing happened. Ric showed up with more things Alice had bought, and he and my mother played cards again. Mom seemed quite happy being able to pick out whatever she wanted from Ric's growing inventory. I was happy when he arrived as my mother had started drinking more heavily and slept much of the day. Playing cards and watching television with Ric got her out of bed and dressed. Since he didn't like how much she drank, he helped to curb her alcohol consumption.

Monday, Ric was a no-show, so I figured that would be the end of his surprise visits, but I was wrong. This time, Ric arrived on Tuesday afternoon to watch a movie with my mom. I was a little miffed that he would continue to show up unasked. When I complained to my mother, she informed me that Ric had been a guest—she had invited him as she was starting to enjoy Ric's company.

That's when I realized what was happening. It wasn't simply that Ric couldn't stand being alone in the house without Alice, although that was certainly the case. Something was starting up between my dead stepmother's third husband and my mom. Why would I be surprised?

Mom stayed at my place, caring for the house and dogs, and we went to Dallas for a wedding in mid-December. I called her to see how she was doing, and there was no answer. I was slightly concerned, but she answered when I called again the next day. When asked where she'd been, she said, "Oh, Ric took me to Pasadena to see all the Christmas lights."

Mom remained with us over Christmas, and on Christmas Eve, Ric came with so many gifts it took him several trips from the car to get them in and under the tree. As was our tradition, we went to church together. I looked down the row at the new couple, and it was evident by the look on Ric's face that he was utterly enamored with my mother. I could read my mother like a book and knew that while she wasn't smitten, she was delighted with the attention, companionship, and gifts Ric was showering on her.

Christmas Day came and went without incident; I think because Mom and Ric were discreet, and it wouldn't occur to anyone, not even Evelyn, that after years of knowing each other, Ric and Mom would hook up so quickly after Alice's passing.

Rather than Mom staying at my place as usual, she and Ric left the next day. Four days later, he took her to a casino for her eighty-first birthday. We all got together for New Year's Eve, but Ric invited her to his place on New Year's Day to watch the Rose Parade on his big-screen TV. She went over and never left.

Mom visited me a few days later and gave me an update. "I watched the Rose Parade with Ric, and he asked me to move in the very next day. I told him I would consider living with him, but I wanted a diamond ring first."

"Good for you, Mom. Make him work for you!"

She smiled. She still had it. I was thrilled for her but also rolled my eyes.

Later that afternoon, Ric showed up with more gifts for my mother. He had an eighteen-karat gold chain, earrings, two purses, and a watch. He forgot the ring! My mother was not amused. But he soon made up for his lapse in memory. The next time I saw them, she had a ring on her finger. After all these years and so many men, she finally got what she wanted at eighty-one—a man who doted on her. He wouldn't let her do a thing. He made her feel like Queen Betty.

Mom and Ric shared a grand love affair. My mother had waited all her life for a man like Ric—someone who loved her without making any demands. I supported her in her happiness. Who was I to judge her? She was genuinely joyful—something I'd never seen in her before.

In the final season of our mom's life, my brother and I stepped up our caregiving efforts after Ric's passing. Her last years were in a retirement community one mile from my home in Covina.

Grateful for the healing process I had walked through with Dr. Gladys years earlier, I was free to choose to love her. I prayed for her. I served her. I really loved her. But, honestly, I did the right thing for her much of the time, aware that I was giving her what she had never been able to provide me with. I became the mother to her that I had needed her to be for me.

Mom's fragility was so prominent that the card games and breakfasts after church stopped. In her way, when she conceded to cooperate with medical advice, she was making amends with me as best she could. Amidst many of her requests, stories, and physical discomfort, she referenced some of the chaos and pain she created. Eric would swing by and spend some time with his Grandma. When visiting her, I brought her fresh roses from my garden. Perched on the side table, she loved them. There, in her senior living apartment, I drank in the fragrance of the roses, absorbing her message and searing these moments of sweet conversation into my memory.

I became the mother to her that I had needed her to be for me.

In 2010, my mother spent her last months in and out of San Dimas Hospital. Allie and I were in regular communication. His medical expertise helped bridge my understanding of her kidney failure, heart issues, and discussions of her decline with the medical staff. In those final weeks, I was at her hospital bedside twice a day, always in frequent conversation with the nurses and doctors involved in her care. I was determined to be there with her when the end came, not missing the sacred moment of her transition from life, as had sadly happened with Dad.

Mom left the hospital to be in hospice at a local care facility. Allie made every effort to be with her when the day came, but she died before he arrived. I was with her while she was hooked up to machines, beeping and cords everywhere. Propped up in her bed, Mom wore a mask for oxygen, and IVs were set up for fluids and her comfort. I grabbed her hand, and she squeezed mine back weakly. Unable to speak, she looked at me with her penetrating eyes. She was scared. I felt her fear. I'd known her fear all my life. I was determined not to let her die in fear. Without thinking, I began to sing. Her favorite hymns were "Amazing Grace" and "Lord, I Am Not Worthy." I felt her hand relax and saw her eyes glisten with tears.

I needed to stand up and stretch. As I left her side, I leaned into the wall in the hallway and cried. Big sobs muffled into my jacket. I hated her for so long, yet now I loved and would miss her. But I also wished her freedom from the duress she was suffering.

So many feelings overtake a person as you watch a loved one fade from this world. I battled my inner child and mature adult parts simultaneously. By her side, I kept returning to singing. It soothed us both.

She stopped seeing me as her body was shutting down. Her face still held the tension of fear. In my heart, I prayed, "Please, Lord! Help her with her fear."

I kept singing, "Was blind, but now I see…"

Shifting her gaze to the upper corner of the room, her face finally relaxed. Mom seemed to smile. Clearly, she saw something I couldn't see. It was in another dimension. I believe it was Dad, there to welcome her, to displace her fear, and to guide her to eternal peace.

Her heart stopped. She was finally liberated from the anxiety and tensions she had battled daily. She could know peace, free from her coping mechanism of chaos. I let go of her hand.

Allie arrived about twenty minutes after she had died. We held each other in a rare moment of affection and connection.

The memories are hazy. I know we signed forms and thanked the staff. Our stoic Swedish roots guided us through the decisions and needed conversations.

I felt ill myself. Nauseous. Light headed. Once in my car and alone, I cried freely. Exhaling, guttural sobs emerged that I'd held inside. "Mom, I miss you! Lord, take care of her and comfort Allie. Dad, thank you for welcoming her home."

The weeks, months, and years after her death braided together the imprint of her life on mine. The wounding, the chaos, and the companionship she brought to my life made it colorful while exhausting and painful. Her fear permeated every moment of her life, and often without awareness, I shouldered that fear for her. I sat staring at the rose bushes in my yard that provided so many filled vases, a prop of love and concern, time and time again. The relief created some guilt, but was quickly replaced by the void.

Mom's death forced me to relinquish my role as the parent of a parent, as one to untangle the knots of self-created drama, as one to walk alongside. I walked a different path because I refused to live in the fear I could have inherited from my mom. I helped her release her fear as she passed on, but she never knew what living in trust and confidence was like.

Committed to learning and growing, I reviewed the love and pain we shared. I look back on my life from this vantage point and am so grateful that Aunt Gertrude stepped in when my mother could not parent. I see how important it was for Lillian to give me a place to belong and confidence in my business skills and abilities. When I was ready, Vanessa offered clarity and insight into myself and the toxic dynamics of my marriage. And, to finally free me from the resentment in my own heart and mind, Dr. Gladys lovingly walked me through the process of forgiving Mom.

Having lost my father many years prior and saying goodbye to my mother opened a new era of life for me. I still suffer the scars of the impact she had on my life. Still, I was able to genuinely care for her emotionally, physically, and spiritually before she passed.

Occasionally, I have the experience of smelling roses—though roses aren't nearby. I think it's Mom's supernatural way of telling me she is there. I can't explain it, but I am comforted by the smell and the sweetness associated with her presence. She and I had made our peace.

To You, My Reader

Thank you for letting me share my story with you.

I'm just a girl from Ohio, from a family of humble beginnings that survived the Great Depression, World War II, and the dramatic changes of the late twentieth century. I also had the added challenge of coping with my mother, who suffered from a severe bipolar disorder. Looking back, having lived many years and now into my eighties, I am driven to fulfill my purpose on this earth. I have shared my purpose in this book with you. Here is my prayer: "Use me, Lord."

I feel my steps are guided. My openness to experience, to know, and to be used by God is a theme throughout my adult life. *Because I Knew You Were Mine* is a part of that purpose—to share a glimpse of my life and healing so that you can learn from my pains and joys.

Like some of you, as a child, I was abandoned, neglected, hungry, suicidal, abused, scared, and angry. I had many caregivers, and my primary parent was gone, working over twelve hours a day. Shy and insecure, I still behaved like a mother to my brother and a parent to my parents. Throughout my years, other people's mental illnesses and infidelities were worked around instead of addressed. Smoking, alcohol, and scarcity were the backdrops of many relationships. I lost myself in solitary behaviors, loving to read, endless games of Solitaire, daydreaming, and, as an adult, work. I learned to settle for connection, even if it was costly.

Identifying the toxic natures of Mom and Dan helped me recognize the chaos they created wherever they went. It took a lot of untangling messages and revealing secrets to see I wasn't solely to blame for the pain I knew. Abandonment and rejection kept replaying until I saw the truth.

Healing, like light, shone on the darkness of rejection, neglect, and abandonment in healthy relationships. Aunt Gertrude saved my young life, literally. She was my loving parent for most of my first five years. She remained a touch point throughout my life. Dad fought for custody of me and Allie. He certainly cared for me and my brother.

I was blessed with mentors that subsidized my lack of parental nurturance. Lillian, my boss at LA Die Mold, recognized my potential and nurtured me to succeed as a young adult. My therapist, Vanessa, patiently listened as grief compounded from my dissolving marriage, single parenting, and the deaths of Dad and Aunt Gertrude, and stresses of running our company paralyzed me. She recognized and comforted my shattered heart. And Dr. Gladys, a medical doctor and national expert on alternative health care provided treatment for my body and my spirit. She guided me toward emotional and physical freedom.

These women were part of the many who were brought into my life to help me heal. Part of my success in life is due to never pushing help away. I received love where and when it was given and grieved where it wasn't. I needed love. I took it in, and it saturated my heart. Little by little, my heart learned to trust, recognize safe people, and mutually give and receive. If you struggle with knowing who to trust, proceed cautiously, but do proceed. No one loves us perfectly. But if we receive what is offered to us, there is love in the world for everyone.

Accepting help and nurture from those who see our pain as well-tilled soil, not as parched discarded ground, restores us.

If I can empathize, I can forgive. – Edgar Cayce

Mom was the most significant source of injury in my life. Her abandonment, fears, chaos, and neediness are woven into so much of my history. To make it confusing, she seldom provided support and love. For any of you harboring similar wounds, it is understandable that you want to stay angry. However, a life of resentment is crippling, and any bitterness isn't worth its weight on your soul.

Mom lived in fear all the time. Her choices were a constant thread of panic, self-soothing, avoiding, manipulating, or chaos-making. I occasionally fell into these traps, too, trying to survive. But, I learned to name my fears, not avoid them. When I put them out in front of me, I am able to move beyond them. I choose to live in love, not fear.

I have asked for help and reinforcement. In order to deal with the next indicated steps, I must avoid turmoil. Change has happened within me. Letting Mom's fears and choices stay hers and not mine freed me from repetitive pain. I can care for and empathize with others, and stay me.

When ye are prepared for a thing, the opportunity to use it presents itself. – Edgar Cayce

The apex of my healing came when I actively forgave my mother at the age of fifty-seven. I prepared myself for years before then to be able to forgive her. And when the opportunity presented itself in the form of the Phoenix women's group with Dr. Gladys, I was ready. The arduous internal work, soul searching, and group processes led me into a new life unimpaired by the weightiness of all things Betty.

Because of this act of forgiveness, I experienced transforming and amazing grace and freedom to be healthy. As a consequence, I can be my own person, rather than an extension of my mother.

Carrying the weight of another's ill health and poor choices will become an open wound. There is no freedom found in that state and you deserve better. Seek out the help you need to get beyond the burden you live with. Prepare yourself and walk into opportunities for healing; seek them out. Be ready to live your life freely.

I have discovered that material possessions do not fulfill me. Instead, I want freedom, health, and purpose. I want things invisible. I also want a hug. Dr. Gladys, who has shown me the invisible, is a living saint, and she always offers me a hug.

> The more knowledge, the more responsibility. The more love, the more ability. – Edgar Cayce

Be aware that your life has purpose. It's up to us to seek out that purpose, knowing we matter as we are. Find a place to belong and to join a community. Let go of your ego, and bring humility and a good heart to your family, work, and passions.

One of the ways I fulfill my purpose is through the charities and non-profit groups I support. Serving on the board of Covenant House, my voice and experience are valued. I started forty-eight years ago giving $2 a month to Covenant House where homeless and trafficked youth are given safety, housing, and guidance. My financial contributions have increased over the years, and I have served on their leadership board.

It is my vocation to provide belonging and facilitate community to anyone with wounds similar to mine. I love to visit and speak with the formerly incarcerated women at Crossroads in Claremont, sharing messages from my first book, *Lady You Got Balls: The Gift of Being Underestimated*. I hope that I serve as a nurturing mother figure to those I encounter at Covenant House and Crossroads.

I support Emanate Health Hospitals, Rotary Club, and other charities. Attending St. Louise Parish, I sing in the choir, filling in as director when needed. I still request the choir to sing "Amazing Grace" as often as possible.

Four of five weekdays, I still go to the company Dan and I started almost fifty years ago. I keep a watchful eye on Eric, production, and morale. I still run to the bank and pay attention to the payables and receivables.

I have always enjoyed traveling and recently have had adventures to North Carolina, Arizona, and Hawaii. But I must admit that after many trips worldwide, the comfort of home and my garden increasingly delight me. That is because my days are scheduled with people, sharing meals, listening well, and nurturing dreams. I communicate privately with the many people brought into my path with need. It is an honor to help families and individuals benefit from what I freely give, with no strings attached.

For all prayer is answered. Don't tell God
how to answer it. – Edgar Cayce

If there is any one message I would want you to take away from this book, it's this: Live open to seeing God in this world. If we are too busy or let our cynicism take root, we will overlook what is right in front of us. And I believe that the more practice seeing through our spiritual eyes, the more God reveals to us.

The last story I will tell you illustrates this point. One Sunday morning, my husband Bill and I were in the choir loft. We stood to sing, and I saw smoke rising from the pews. I was outraged. How dare someone smoke in church. I tried to stand on my tiptoes and get a look, but as I sat in the third row back, I still couldn't see anything. The smoke seemed to be coming from the back pews, just right of center, right in front of me. I looked around, but no one else seemed to notice, or if they did, they didn't consider it important. I thought everyone would be just as outraged as I was when they did see the smoke.

We sat down. A few minutes later, we stood again and then knelt. I saw more smoke. This guy must be smoking a cigar! I wondered why I didn't hear people milling about. Why aren't the people beside him drumming him out of the church? The choir still didn't seem to notice. I looked at my husband sitting next to me. He didn't seem to notice anything out of the ordinary either. Now, I was beginning to wonder about myself. Why don't I smell the cigar smoke? I was getting concerned. Am I really seeing this?

There was a lot of smoke rising now, like a big column. I removed my glasses, thinking this must be a reflection of the inside of my glasses. The lighting wasn't good up there. No, even without my glasses, I could still see the smoke. Some of it had risen to the ceiling and was easier to see against the dark wood. I even thought I might be seeing a reflection on the glass windows from a car driving by. No, that can't be. I've never seen a reflection like that before.

I was so concerned about what I was seeing. The choir stood and sang another song, but I went through the motions. We sat back down. Is there something wrong with my eyes? Am I crazy?

Suddenly, the whole column started to swirl, slowly at first and then faster and faster, tighter and tighter. I could see it now against the dark ceiling. I also wanted to tell Bill to watch it, but I didn't dare take my eyes off the smoke.

I hadn't noticed, but the Holy Communion had begun. Just as Father Dennis Young held up the wafer, the smoke shot straight down and into the altar. I saw it clearly against the dark ceiling but almost lost sight of it as it passed the gray brick walls at the back of the altar. I was in awe. The service ended, and Bill and I walked out together. I asked if he'd seen it, and he hadn't, so I dropped the conversation.

What have I seen? Did I really see it? And if I did, why? I pondered this experience many times. I tried to talk with Bill, but he didn't understand. Finally, I decided to share my vision in a letter with Monseigneur Pierce. I followed up with a visit in his office. Shockingly, when we spoke, he wasn't surprised at all by what I'd experienced. He said something I'll never forget. "You have been given the grace to see this, Pat."

In searching for a reason for this unique happening, the impression repeatedly was to strengthen my faith. It was my chance to see the unseen momentarily. The sense of an angel on my shoulder, the guidance of my steps, and glimpses of God were for my eyes only. May you have eyes to see God's grace and belonging, however it manifests for you.

P.S. And eighty years later, I still hate beets.

Epilogue

(In order of appearance.)

Patricia Stroberg

Sitting in my beautiful home with friends and family close by, I have realized my many dreams. I freed myself from a toxic marriage and finally got the chance to become the businesswoman I was meant to be. I have traveled the world, delighting in places, people, and cultures. But my most important accomplishments are matters of the heart, soul, and spirit.

Marilyn

My cousin, Marilyn, and her delightful husband, Tom, still live in Ohio. She holds the most shared history with me of anyone on this planet. We travel together to Hawaii and Florida or take in the fall colors in the northeast. No matter where we are, many hours pass playing Hand and Foot card game.

Allie

My brother Al retired from his medical practice and, with his wife, tends to his orchards on the Central Coast. Their two sons have families of their own, and we all wish we could gather more often.

Dan

Dan and I had kept our distance from one another since our divorce was finalized in 1985. During the writing of the final pages of this manuscript, I was informed of his death from a heart attack. He was eighty-five years old.

Lillian and the Schwarz Family

I stayed in touch with Lillian and her family for many years and was included in their celebrations and events as family. They have all since passed away, but they are alive in my memories. My life was changed by the impact of their love and support. I hope every employer can understand the positive influence that can be achieved by treating employees with respect and kindness.

Eric

Eric is based loosely on my son. He, his wife, and two sons live near me, often sharing Sunday breakfasts and taking in Netflix series. Being Eric's mother is still the greatest happiness I know. Since his birth, he has been the light of my life.

Eric runs the family business now. The success of our company has been constant, with loyal employees, good products, and profit. I am proud and honored that my son is now in charge, though I still keep a frequent check on the pulse of the company. In the decades with a woman leading the business, its tone and health were transformed for the betterment of our employees, customers, and our bottom line.

A more detailed story of my marriage, taking over the family business, and, eventually, turning the reins over to my son is told in my first book, *Lady You Got Balls: The Gift of Being Underestimated*, available on Amazon or your local bookstore.

Sophie

Sophie—the neighbor who shared many intellectual and spiritual awakenings with me when my son was young—and I have stayed in touch for sixty-plus years. And she now lives in the apartment above my garage. Sophie has a green thumb and keeps our large garden alive with color and tranquility.

Vanessa

A vibrant and gifted therapist, Vanessa's life ended too early at the age of fifty-four due to illness. I can still hear her voice in my mind, encouraging me, guiding me, showing me the way. She arrived in my life at just the right time.

Bill

Bill, the love of my life, gave me great joy and showed me what it was like to be loved by a good man. Unfortunately, he was a smoker and, despite trying to quit, passed away from lung cancer in 1996 at the age of sixty-nine. But his love is fresh in my heart even to this day.

Dr. Gladys McGarey

Gratefully, Dr. Gladys McGarey and I are still in contact. We meet as friends three times a year, and I cherish the learning I gain at every encounter. Today, at one hundred and two, as the mother of holistic medicine, Dr. Gladys just celebrated publishing her most recent book, sharing her wisdom in *The Well-Lived Life: A 102-Year-Old Doctor's Six Secrets to Health and Happiness at Every Age.*

About the Author

Born in Cleveland, Ohio, in 1940 and raised there, Pat still sees herself as "Just a girl from Ohio." Quickly, from her writing, you learn there is a lot more to this upbeat, confident, and sharp woman. She moved to California as a teen, married at nineteen, became a mother at twenty-two, a company co-owner at thirty-one, and its president at forty-five.

Pat's childhood was lonely, sad, and filled with loss. Parented by her emotionally distant father and abandoned by her mother, Pat's extended family and paid caregivers provided the sense of belonging needed by a young girl.

After finishing high school, she married the boy next door. To their delight, they had a son a few years later. The couple started a manufacturing business in the plastics industry. Pat worked almost every position in that company at one time or another, and their business flourished.

Her marriage and starting their company filled some missing emotional pieces initially. Still, it proved to repeat many of the pains of her childhood. After twenty-six years of marriage, emotionally battered and seeking a light at the end of the tunnel, Pat divorced her husband. After becoming the sole owner of the company, Pat excelled as its president and transformed it into a multi-million-dollar business. She cracked the glass ceiling and became an esteemed member of the "Top 100 Women-Owned Businesses in Southern California."

Pat became an author at eighty-two, writing her stories for others to read. Her first book, *Lady You Got Balls*, and the latest, *Because I Knew You Were Mine,* grew out of a daily journal Pat kept since she was sixteen. Pat's honest, candid, relatable, and humorous accounts reveal a raw journey through emotional anguish, trauma, financial success, and healing.

Curiosity and a love of adventure still characterize Pat's life. Books, mentors, employees, colleagues, travel, and spiritual wisdom keep her growing. Her purpose, efficiency, and generosity stem from these. Providing leadership, guidance, and loyalty to many individuals and profit and non-profit organizations has been a constant thread throughout her adult life.

Pat lives with her dog and several visiting friends at her Covina Hills home. She loves spending time with her son, daughter-in-law, and two grandsons. She plays bridge, travels, and sings in her parish choir. And she still writes in her journal daily.

Note from the Publisher

We at Berry Powell Press are extremely proud to publish this complex and compelling story rooted in Patricia Stroberg's personal experience.

It's accurate to say that Pat embodies the values we hold at Berry Powell Press. She has overcome challenges that could have overwhelmed any one of us. Rather than choosing to shut down in the face of betrayal and abandonment, Pat remained open to whatever goodness God sent her way. Her resilient faith, unquenchable curiosity, and indomitable determination to find out the truth propelled her well beyond the trajectory of her childhood.

While many readers will not have suffered abandonment and abuse to the extent that was inflicted on Pat, her story rings true for anyone who has struggled with their relationships with their parents. Her father was protective but emotionally distant. Yet Pat's deepest wounds were inflicted by her mother, who was also deeply troubled by past abuse and mental health issues.

But the book doesn't leave readers in despair by any means. Instead, Pat's story is a lifeline to hope and healing. We offer *Because I Knew You Were Mine* to the many who desperately need this message. In doing so, we fulfill the purpose of our publishing house—to launch books that have the power to inspire healing and the opportunity to thrive.

If you have a message that needs to become a book, please visit our website at www.berrypowellpress.com.

Berry Powell Press is a hybrid publishing house that publishes authors with transformational perspectives on timely personal and societal challenges. We provide our authors with in-depth mentorship and collaborative assistance to create life-changing books. Additionally, we assist them in building book-based businesses that can impact the largest audience possible. We publish fiction and non-fiction for adults and children.

www.ingramcontent.com/pod-product-compliance
Lightning Source LLC
LaVergne TN
LVHW020926090426
835512LV00020B/3219